SERVING LIFE

BEHIND BARS, KITCHENS, AND HOSPITALITY

Justin Michael Morales

DEDICATION

To my OG family, my industry family, and my new family, Sam and Winslow. I am blessed for how I became who I am and for what I am to become.

There is so much love I need to repay.

ACKNOWLEDGMENTS

I'd like to thank Amy Silver White for her thorough proofreading. Thank you to Patricia Harris & David Lyon for the wonderful advice. A special thanks to Ben Dubow for bringing me into the fold at Forge City Works, a place that provides purpose to an old line cook. I am grateful to the talented photographers Winter Caplanson, Lisa Nichols, and Michael Leungevity for sharing your talents with the world. Thanks to Erik Ofgang and Dana Slone for not laughing when I said I wanted to write and for providing invaluable guidance. Thank you, industry pros that came before me, accepted me, and taught me what hard work can do. Thank you, industry pros on the rise who continue to teach me we can change the game for the better. Thank you to the Connecticut Restaurant Association for light-housing us through Covid. Lastly, thank you to every cut and burn I have received. I'll never forget you.

FOREWORD

I've known Justin Morales for nearly a decade and a half, and if you had told me back then that he'd become one of my closest friends and most respected colleagues, I might have laughed. In those early days, Justin rubbed me the wrong way–he seemed arrogant, demanding, a bit of an ass, if I'm being honest. As a line cook at a suburban Hartford restaurant, I often found myself on the receiving end of his special requests and his occasional outbursts if something wasn't to his liking.

At first glance, I mistook him for a manager due to his commanding presence. However, I soon learned that he was just a bartender, albeit one with an intense dedication to ensuring every guest left with a smile. Justin wasn't being difficult for the sake of it; he was passionate about hospitality, about the craft of serving behind bars. Once I grasped this, my opinion of him shifted, and a mutual respect blossomed. We both shared a profound connection to the restaurant world–a world that would ultimately shape our lives in ways we never anticipated.

Over the years, Justin and I have collaborated on various ventures, from opening restaurants to consulting and hosting a podcast. Now, we embark on a project that holds special meaning: empowering individuals facing barriers to employment through the transformative power of food and hospitality.

There's something inherently redemptive about this industry, a sentiment Justin eloquently explores in these pages. He recounts how it saved him, instilling in him a sense of purpose and a calling beyond himself. I can attest to similar experiences.

Serving Life: Behind Bars, Kitchens, and Hospitality is Justin's story, but it's also a story shared by many of us who have found solace and meaning within the confines of kitchens and dining rooms. Whether you've toiled in hospitality or simply enjoyed a drink at the bar, Justin's narrative offers a glimpse into a world both familiar and enlightening.

Justin is not just a skilled bartender; he's one of the finest hospitality professionals I've had the pleasure of knowing. He's a masterful storyteller and, above all, a good human being.

So, as you embark on this journey through the vibrant world of bars and restaurants, I invite you to savor every page, raise a toast to the indomitable spirit of hospitality, and embrace the camaraderie that binds us all.

Bon appétit, salut, and here's to the journey ahead!

Ben Dubow

HARTFORD, CT

2024

Pre-Shift

My journey through the hospitality industry began when I was just seventeen years old, armed with nothing but naivety, wanderlust, and no map. Growing up dyslexic, feral, financially challenged, and surrounded by adults addicted to drugs and all kinds of stunted intellect, I had already started a few steps back from the starting line of life. But it was within the walls of the kitchen that I found not just my stride but my true path.

This book is an exploration of the life's journey I embarked upon in the hospitality industry, but it's also a celebration of the countless talented and unique individuals who, like me, have found their place within this extraordinary world. We are the chefs, servers, bartenders, and operators who thrive in the chaos, revel in the camaraderie, and cherish the diversity that defines our profession.

As I recount my experiences from that small coffee shop kitchen to bustling New York City bars, from the art of sautéing to shaking up award-winning cocktails, you'll come to understand the passion that drives us. But this journey isn't about culinary and cocktail expertise alone; it's a deeper exploration of the hospitality community's values, culture, and unspoken bonds.

In *Serving Life: Behind Bars, Kitchens, and Hospitality*, you'll discover lessons learned in the heat of the kitchen, the joys of celebrating diversity, and the unique challenges we face from misconceptions held by those outside our industry, aka civilians. You'll also witness the behind-the-scenes moments of training people with employment barriers, navigating tough hours, and dealing with addiction issues and mental health struggles in the restaurant business. We are the island of misfit toys.

But above all, this book is a tribute to the unbreakable spirit that defines us as hospitality professionals. It's an ode to the "club" we've all joined, where backgrounds, education, and origins matter little. Here, we all start at the same spot in the race, and those who can keep up reap the rewards, knowing that we do our jobs better than anyone else.

So, as you embark on this up-and-down journey with me, I invite you to step into our world, to understand what truly makes us tick, and to appreciate the artistry, dedication, and heart that go into each plate and every smile. It's time to unveil the secrets hidden behind the uniform and celebrate the extraordinary individuals who make every dining experience memorable.

In this book, you'll encounter stories marked with a (SIDE QUEST) label. These are extended versions of the tales told throughout the pages. If a particular story piques your interest and you find yourself craving a deeper dive, just flip to the back of the book. There, the SIDE QUESTS will be waiting, offering a more comprehensive and detailed exploration of the adventures and experiences that have shaped my journey.

Welcome to the world of *Serving Life: Behind Bars, Kitchens, and Hospitality*.

CONTENTS

Chapter One	Embracing The Flames	1
Chapter Two	Chaotic Compass	8
Chapter Three	Burners, Mise en Place, and Camaraderie	15
Chapter Four	Crossroads and Choices	24
Chapter Five	From City to City to City	34
Chapter Six	Lost And Found	49
Chapter Seven	Behind The Bar	57
Chapter Eight	Raising The Bar	64
Chapter Nine	Pearls In The Oyster	73
Chapter Ten	The Chinese Proverb	81
Chapter Eleven	Crafting A Career	87
Chapter Twelve	Anyone Know A Chef?	93
Chapter Thirteen	Behind The Music	101
Chapter Fourteen	Spring Cleaning	109
Chapter Fifteen	Going In Blind	115
Chapter Sixteen	Crying In The Walk-In	122
Chapter Seventeen	Resurrecting A Ghost	128
Chapter Eighteen	A Zero's Journey	134
Chapter Nineteen	Navigating The Real Storm	140
Chapter Twenty	Savor Every Up And Down	146
Chapter Twenty One	Tio And The Nighthawk	151
Chapter Twenty Two	The Call Back	155
Chapter Twenty Three	Born Again	158
Chapter Twenty Four	The Mission	162
Chapter Twenty Five	Win, Lose, Win	166
EOD	End Of Day	170
Side Quest 1	Across Country – 1994 - Age 19	174
Side Quest 2	Across The Pond – 1996 - Age 21	183
Side Quest 3	Busking The System – 2011 - Age 31	197
Drink Recipes	Beso Roja	205
	Filthy Rich	206
	Kiss From a Rose	207
	Omotenashitni	208
	Nightrider	209
	The Secretariat	210
	Yuzu Cowboy	211
	(CCCC) California Coast Cucumber Crush	212
	Louisville Sour	213

CHAPTER ONE

EMBRACING THE FLAMES

Angel and I were deeply engaged in conversation about the business and what he could accomplish with hard work. Angel was 52 and I was 48. He shared that he had spent over 30 years in prison and was thrilled to be participating in our training program, on track to become an intern and, hopefully, a full-time line cook at a livable wage. His work ethic was undeniable–diligent, generous, and kind. The program we offered seemed to be making a real difference for him, and in turn, his progress was profoundly affecting me. It was a form of mutual healing. Despite being roughly the same age, I found it ironic that I sported far more tattoos than he did. If you didn't know who we were, you might think we swapped roles. Angel was navigating his way out of three decades behind prison bars, embarking on a promising new path with us. In parallel, after more than 30 years working behind bars and kitchens and navigating the hospitality world, I was embracing a new chapter of my life as well. Though our paths were very different, they had intersected in this restaurant, drawing us together on a shared journey.

When I was two weeks old, I had pneumonia. I'm not one to wallow in self-pity, but in retrospect, there's no better metaphor for my introduction to this world—a fight from the first breath. This struggle was more than just a health battle; it was a prelude to a life where challenges were the norm, not the exception. From my early days navigating through chaos and poverty to the heat of the kitchen, each step was a battle, each victory a testament to resilience.

I grew up in the north end of Manchester, Connecticut, in the early '80s. My mother, just 16 when she had me, raised me in a predominantly blue-collar, Polish, and Lithuanian neighborhood. The landmark Kelly's Pub was right across the street—the queen of all dive bars, a standout amidst the residential houses. Sissy, a true spitfire, ran the pub after Kelly's passing. I think she may be 140 years old today and still working—I wouldn't be surprised. Both my aunt and mother worked there at one point, adding to its significance for me. Everyone knew everyone. I remember attending my first keg party in the woods when I was four or five years old, which was fun. I was surrounded by 19- to 22-year-olds having fun around a fire, and I was the adored mascot.

As a child, I adored the neighborhood. It was a place without fences, an endless playground where I could get lost in adventures until the sun started to set. That's when either I or one of my friends would eventually hear a loud yell: "InsertNameHere, COME HOME NOW!" As I grew older, I began to realize how much this environment, as endearing as it was in many ways, played a large part in the hardships I would face throughout my life.

Living with my grandmother, another single mother, I started to see the world differently as I grew. Our environment was steeped in addiction and toxic behavior. The instability was constant—I attended five different elementary schools and three middle schools as we moved around. My mother often disappeared into rehab clinics. My life was a patchwork of various family dynamics, ranging from nurturing to outright abusive.

For the longest time, I didn't even realize my life was tough. Hunger, fear, and loneliness seemed normal until I discovered what it meant to have a full belly, security, and friendship. I straddled these two worlds throughout my life, yet I never fully blamed anyone for my hardships. I could have resented my stepfather for his psychological torment or my mother for prioritizing her addiction over me, but I chose not to. Instead, I found solace with my aunt Linda and uncle Bruce during my mother's rehab stints. They provided a moral compass and a stable home, offering something I'd never had before–boundaries. It wasn't easy fitting into their life; I was a troubled child, a true rescue. But over time, their influence became my salvation.

Linda, my mother's sister, had broken free from the cycle of abuse and addiction that plagued our family and neighborhood, thanks to Bruce. Bruce, belonging to a conservative Irish background, was expected to excel academically and behave. While he had his wild streak, he always met his obligations, albeit in his own unique way. Together, Linda and Bruce were a stable couple, sadly unable to have children of their own. At times, I became their surrogate child, and, I can assure you, I didn't make it easy on them. Their stability was a contrast to my usual life that brought a newfound maturity, even at six years old.

I remember one Easter when my mother was in rehab, and I was staying with Linda and Bruce. She came to visit, bringing an Easter card, which I later found in her car. In a mix of anger and pain I didn't fully comprehend, I ripped up the card and left it there. When she discovered the torn card, her tears taught me a painful lesson: hurting someone you love out of spite doesn't balance the scales. It was at the tender age of six that I learned to forgive. Forty-two years later, that wound remains the freshest in my memory.

While home was a patchwork of tough experiences, school presented its own set of challenges and lessons. It was another world I had to navigate, my first interaction with what I perceived as "normal" humans. They didn't seem normal but I suppose I didn't either. The left-handed scissors and a free lunch ticket were only the beginning. As an observer, academic subjects came easily to me until the fourth grade. That's when dyslexia reared its head with full force. Struggling with reading, I started acting out in class. Part of it was embracing the anger stemming from feeling different; I had been to friends' houses and had seen family dynamics vastly different from my own. My grades plummeted from easy A's to D's, and visits to the principal's office became a routine. I preferred flirting with girls and pissing off teachers rather than facing the embarrassment of reading difficulties. At home and at school, no one recognized the root of my behavioral changes; I was just labeled the bad kid. In a way, I didn't mind that label. When I hit high school, I spent much time in Saturday school, detention, and in-school suspension. The company I kept during these pockets of time were my teachers in very different subjects. This helped me understand people from all walks of life. This pattern persisted until my senior year when I was asked to leave school. I was indifferent to being kicked out, but as you can imagine, my aunt and uncle were far from pleased. "If you're not going to school, you're getting a job," they said. "No problem," I said.

Working gave me a new perspective on food, transforming it from a mere necessity to an experience. At school, I received free lunch, which was both noticeable and embarrassing. At home, culinary delights were rare. My mother, limited by our financial situation and sometimes not even being present or awake, occasionally treated me to McDonald's on welfare day. My meals were simple: generic mac 'n' cheese or shake 'n' bake. On the rare occasions we had brand-name versions, it felt like a feast. Our pantry was filled with nondescript food boxes labeled "White bread," "Peanut butter," or in the fridge, "Cheese." Eating was functional, not pleasurable. Yet, there were moments of unexpected joy. A simple meal like fried bologna with melted cheese on fresh white bread was surprisingly satisfying. The crispy bologna, gooey cheese, and soft bread created a symphony of textures and flavors, a rare delight in my otherwise bland culinary world. Most of the time, I had to be creative with limited ingredients. I made toast with mayonnaise, burning it slightly for extra flavor in the absence of butter. My version of "Italian food" was white bread with tomato sauce and American cheese. I prided myself on being the best "poor man's chef" at the age of seven.

It wasn't until I stayed with my aunt and uncle that I experienced more substantial and healthy meals, though they were often bland and just not really my thing. Their menu typically featured dishes like boiled meat and wheat bread and dried cranberries—hardly enticing to a young palate. However, there was a silver lining: Friday-night pizzas. We indulged in Greek-style pepperoni and hamburger pizza from Midway, a glorious treat that made Fridays my favorite day, lasting until I landed my first job in a kitchen.

A notable blessing came during a stint around the age of 15 or 16 when I stayed with my good friend Dave and his family. His mother was a single parent of three; a hardworking, wonderful human who cooked the best Puerto Rican food I had ever tasted. My favorite was *pernil*, delicious slow-roasted pork with Spanish rice and beans. Even better was the scorched rice at the bottom of the pot, known as *pegao*. These meals stood in stark contrast to the ones at Linda and Bruce's, adding a much-needed variety to my culinary experiences.

Work became my sanctuary, a place where I felt in control and the master of my own destiny, even at the young age of ten. I always had a paper route, but as a child, that income was only enough for the occasional candy bar or Twinkies. My first substantial job was working in the tobacco fields. At 15, I became the assistant to an older Jamaican man who sang Motown songs to the crew, with a reggae twist. His music was infectious, making the long hours under the sun more bearable. I still remember receiving my first real paycheck–it felt like a fortune. With the hard-earned $105, I indulged in a feast of food delivery: Chinese food, calzones, and pizzas, all in one sitting. Three different delivery guys arriving at the same time were very perplexed. For the first time, I ate like a god, experiencing what it was like to have more than enough. That meal was a revelation–it wasn't until much later that I truly understood that gods indeed ate much better. My belly was ridiculously full, but it was more than just physical satisfaction; it was a taste of freedom and self-sufficiency. I loved that feeling and was determined never to go hungry again. The ability to earn made me feel kingly and ready to venture out into the world–to explore and to eat. Hunger had once made me feel helpless; now, the ability to quell it made me fearless.

Now that I was working, I began to view all my usual hangouts as potential sources of income. It was during this time that I stumbled upon my first kitchen job. There was a coffee shop where my stoner friends and I used to hang out–a place that tolerated just about anything from underage kids. The owners, an older couple, not only ran the coffee shop but also supplemented their income by selling pot to us. We spent so much time there, it almost felt like we were adopted by them, reminiscent of a ragtag gang of Cockney pickpockets from *Oliver Twist*. Among us, I was probably the most feral, and the owners noticed that quickly. I was on the cusp of 17 when they offered me a job to run their kitchen, driven more by their license requirements than my culinary skills. They paid me a salary of $117 a week, sometimes. In addition to this, I also sold weed for them. I clocked in over 50 hours a week, initially making turkey sandwiches, until Gordon came along.

Gordon was a man 30 years my senior with genuine kitchen experience. My new boss. His face bore the scars of a major kitchen fire; skin regrafted in a patchwork of survival and resilience. Despite his appearance, Gordon was incredibly kind and became my unexpected mentor. He taught me recipes I didn't even know I wanted to learn, like how to make stuffed mushrooms–a dish that would later become part of my claim to fame and a stepping-stone to many more cooking jobs. I relished the process of creating something from an idea to fruition, seeing the tangible result of my labor on a plate, and then witnessing the joy it brought to someone's face. But the most crucial lesson I learned from Gordon after hearing about his kitchen fire was the importance of safety. That lesson stuck with me more than any recipe. Here I was, about to serve life, and I didn't even know it. Bring on the flames.

CHAPTER TWO

CHAOTIC COMPASS

I worked at the coffee shop for nearly a year until the paychecks began to bounce. Eventually, the owners shut it down and attempted a rebranding, but word had spread among the local kids to steer clear of employment there, leading to its permanent closure. Leveraging my time at the cafe as a "cooking experience," I managed to secure a job at a chain restaurant near the mall. I entered the job thinking I'd be high on the totem pole, given my previous experience, but I quickly realized I didn't know as much as I thought. Fortunately, the job mainly involved manning the fry station and heating items in the microwave–tasks that required little culinary skill. This was a corporate kitchen, starkly different from what I was used to: the floor was clean and perfectly tiled, equipment filled every corner, along with binders and Sharpies, and rules and regulations plastered the walls. The morning smell of stale fry oil and bleach was unmistakable. As I walked in, I felt the hungry eyes of the kitchen staff sizing me up. It was a new kind of excitement. Although I hadn't aspired to be a cook, it was a skill I could list on my resumé, and so far, it was opening doors for me.

The corporate kitchen was fine, but it wasn't really for me. At that age, I lacked direction and soon realized that kitchens were always in need of help, a fact that seemed to fuel my wanderlust. However, this lack of a clear path led me into trouble. With some money in my pocket, I began gambling, quickly falling into addiction, thanks in part to my step-uncle, who was a bookie. Drinking became a nightly routine. If I didn't feel like working, I'd simply move on to the next kitchen job. I was far from becoming the best version of myself. Anger began to surface more frequently, and the chip on my shoulder grew heavier.

During this period, my hair was long, down to my back, and very unkempt. I was living wherever I could find someone willing to put up with me. My mother, still struggling with her drug addiction, had attempted to end her life, unable to overcome her habit. The responsibility of caring for another child only compounded her guilt and despair. My relationship with my stepfather had deteriorated to the point of physical altercations, marking a new low in our already nasty interactions. To be fair, he was a real dick.

Even my aunt and uncle, who had always been my safety net, were no longer an option. Their approach to tough love clashed with my mindset at the time. I was floating, aimlessly wandering through life, unable to find comfort or stability anywhere.

At 19, I hit rock bottom. Facing a minor arrest warrant and saddled with a $2,000 debt to a bookie–someone other than my uncle, which meant no familial leniency–I found myself in a not-so-good situation. I had left behind any idea of a stable life, not that I even wanted that, propelled by restlessness and desperation.

I sold whatever possessions I had and purchased a bus ticket to Tampa. A friend was living there in an apartment paid for by his parents as he was attending school in the city. He had invited me to visit, and I was ready for an adventure, eager to find something–anything–that might fill the void in my soul.

With a bit of money in my pocket, I set out on my journey, but my financial situation quickly deteriorated. By the time I reached Penn Station in New York City, I learned a tough lesson in the realities of city life. I stuck out like a sore thumb with my long hair and tie-dyed shirt decorated with pot leaves and cargo pants. A smooth-talking con artist swindled me, all under the indifferent eyes of nearby police officers. It was a rude awakening to the harsh ways of the world: don't trust seemingly friendly faces too easily, particularly when their gestures of kindness are unproven.

In my naivety, I had bought oregano, mistaking it for something more lucrative, and fake LSD, hoping to sell them upon my arrival in Tampa. I spent half the trip sweating over these worthless purchases. It's amusing in hindsight, but at the time, it was anything but funny. I remember thinking that if I only possessed the con artist's gift of gab, maybe I could offload this stuff. But as fate would have it, I was soon to develop a similar skill, and perhaps even surpass him in the art of persuasion.

When I arrived in Tampa, the contrast was extreme and instantly captivating. The transition from the oak trees of New England to the palm trees of Florida symbolized a whole new world to me. The sunshine and warmth were a welcomed change, but the most important difference–I didn't see it as much at the time–was discovering the local fast food options. Checkers was a revelation, offering a new style of affordable garbage. Given my limited budget, this brand new fast food was both delicious and necessary.

Eager to dive into this new chapter, I soon realized that the job market in Tampa was markedly different from Connecticut. Finding kitchen work proved challenging, though I must admit my efforts weren't exhaustive. I was looking for something different, a new start. Browsing through the want ads, one particular listing caught my eye: "Looking for a manager. No experience needed; must like having fun in a rock and roll environment with good pay." It seemed like the perfect opportunity for any lost nineteen-year-old. I didn't hesitate to call the number and set up an interview as soon as possible.

I arrived at the interview location, a nondescript storefront in an industrial park. After checking in with the receptionist, I sat down, waiting for what I hoped would be the opportunity of a lifetime. Soon, I was called in and met by a young woman, 23 years old I later learned, attractive and impeccably put together. She exuded authority–a true boss lady.

Our conversation, which lasted about 30 minutes, seemed to revolve around nothing in particular, circling without landing on any specific point. Yet, at the end of it, she announced that I was hired. Surprisingly, I still had no clear idea of what the job entailed. All I grasped was the potential to quickly ascend to a branch manager position and make a substantial amount of money. She seemed genuinely excited to have someone with my "talents," although I wasn't even sure what talents she was referring to at the time.

I left with instructions on where and when to show up for orientation, zooming with excitement despite still being in the dark about the nature of my new job. The orientation was led by Louie, the owner–a charismatic character in his forties with slicked-back hair, a goatee, a noticeable paunch, and a button-up shirt casually opened to reveal a gold chain and chest hair.

I was about to start selling knock-off cologne and perfume. Surrounded by a motley crew who accepted me unconditionally, I didn't mind the oddity of it all. After all, I've always felt a kinship with the unconventional. This job brought together people from all walks of life, united in the same pursuit—another lesson I was soon to realize. So, why not give it a shot? The arrangement was simple: they supplied the product, and I would keep a percentage of my sales. Ironically, I found myself swindled yet again, not even a month later, but at least I saw it for what it was finally. It was high time I figured this out.

After a motivational meeting, I hit the streets, shy and lacking in sales skills. I was kicked out of numerous places, but the need to eat was a powerful motivator. I clung to the goal of enduring the 99 no's to find that one yes, which I learned earlier in the meeting. I approached everyone and entered every business I could. My world changed the day I met an older, sharply dressed black man in the streets of Ybor City. When I asked him to buy some cologne, he laughed, saying I was doing it all wrong. He introduced himself as Lightning and offered to show me the ropes. By then, I was wary of smooth talkers, but I had nothing to lose except the cheap fragrances in my bag.

Reluctantly, I handed him two bottles to show me his technique. I watched in awe as he sold both within minutes to passersby. He then returned the money I owed for the bottles, plus an extra ten bucks, keeping the rest for himself. That day, Lightning taught me a crucial lesson: confidence is key. It's more about the show you put on than the product itself.

He told me to follow him into a trinket store, where he used his earnings to buy fake gold chains. I spent the day shadowing him, absorbing every tactic and maneuver. It was a lesson in hustle, respect for the hustle, and the art of selling.

Taking Lightning's lesson to heart, I started making sales the very next day. I pitched to people at gas stations, storeowners, and mechanics, claiming each bottle was a "guaranteed panty dropper"–not my line, but it worked. As I began earning the respect of Louie and the other misfits, I realized the only real difference between Louie and Lightning was that Lightning had been honest with me.

AJ, a year younger than me and every bit the skater chick, was quirky and refreshingly unconventional. We teamed up to sell cologne and perfume together, and before long, she proposed that we go on a "satellite." In our line of work, a satellite meant taking a large inventory of products from the warehouse and traveling out of the area to sell them. Thanks to her status as a manager, AJ managed to secure a substantial amount upfront, along with a few bottles set aside to cover our expenses. She suggested Kentucky as our destination for this satellite mission, anticipating we'd be gone for a couple of days. The idea of a business trip, regardless of the business, intrigued me. "What the hell," I thought.

Our journey began in her 1975 orange VW Bug, a car held together by duct tape and improvisation, including a pencil repurposed as a car part. I soon discovered that her license was suspended, and the license plate was scavenged from another VW Bug. This was shaping up to be a wild adventure. What was planned as a four-day trip to Kentucky morphed into a two-month odyssey through 14 states. Along the way, we experienced a car fire, a search and seizure, a daring heist to retrieve the car from the police pound, an encounter with the Knoxville Police Department, memorable road music, and a cast of intriguing characters. This was before MapQuest and GPS. Luckily, before I left for Florida, a truck driver neighbor told me if you own a map, you own the world, and I had purchased a road atlas right before we left.

We eventually made our way back to Connecticut, where AJ and I went our separate ways. Neither I, nor the cologne and perfume, ever returned to Tampa. My birthday passed during our journey, marking not just another year of age but also a rebirth of sorts. I had gone on my first odyssey. I was becoming even more fearless and far more thirsty for adventure. (SIDE QUEST #1 CROSS COUNTRY).

CHAPTER THREE

BURNERS, MISE EN PLACE, AND CAMARADERIE

Back in Connecticut, I found myself transformed. Equipped with new tools and a burning passion for travel and hustle, I knew I needed money to fulfill these ambitions. Given that my resume was mostly filled with kitchen work, it seemed logical to return to that field. I landed jobs at various local pizza joints, where I honed skills in prep–from batching meatballs to making dough and slicing veggies. Yet one task was particularly challenging: chopping onions. Onions release a chemical irritant known as syn-propanethial-s-oxide, which triggers a stinging sensation and prompts tears to flush out the irritant. It was sheer torture for me. The older workers suggested myriad methods to protect my eyes, but none worked. I sometimes wondered if they were just amusing themselves by seeing how far I'd go to avoid the torture.

In these kitchens, I learned the art of making marinara sauce and mastered sautéing a few signature dishes. Cooking hundreds of pounds of pasta became a daily routine. Eventually, I joined the team at Nullis Italia, a local favorite owned by Fred Anulli. The place was a booming, traditional Italian restaurant complete with an accordion player, a singer, and a bocce ball court in the back room. Fred, a 75-year-old man, would greet guests at the door with his apron on, offering handshakes and welcoming smiles. His eyes would often wander to the open kitchen, scanning the space with an intense gaze. Being a newcomer, I frequently found myself the target of his scrutiny. He rarely smiled at the staff, reserving his warmth for the guests. His silent, watchful presence was intimidating, and he never addressed me directly, only observing from a distance. I was told this was his usual approach with new staff.

One hectic night, after a particularly challenging dinner service, which I managed to keep pace with, Fred walked past me, gave me a tap on the shoulder, and said, "Good job, Justin." I was almost in disbelief. From that day on, he never stared at me in that way again and always greeted me with a hello. Lesson learned: respect and recognition in this industry have to be earned.

Although working at Nullis was great, the routine eventually started to feel mundane. My thirst for adventure was rekindled when my friend Paul mentioned a trip to Ireland for a cousin's wedding. He and another friend, Ryan, planned to attend the wedding and travel around the U.K. and northern Europe for a few months. At 21, I was eager for new experiences and this sounded exactly like what I needed. The only hitch was my limited budget, which paled in comparison to what Paul and Ryan had for their travels. But undeterred, I decided to take the plunge and see where the journey took me. This adventure alone could fill another book, so I'll have to leave out a lot of details. However, as expected, I quickly ran out of money.

We set up a base camp at a college in Cambridge, England, where we met a South Carolinian student studying abroad. She offered us her tiny room—a cramped space but still an upgrade from our tent. Needing work, I looked for opportunities in local restaurants, knowing I'd have to work under the table due to my lack of a visa. That's how I ended up at the Blue Ox, a pub in downtown Cambridge. My cover story to Chef Andrew was that I'd work as a prep and dishwasher until my "visa came in"–a classic tale in the kitchen world.

The experience at the Blue Ox was nothing short of awesome. I prepared dishes like leek soup, Yorkshire pudding, and lamb burgers–cuisines that were both foreign and intriguing to me. This job rekindled my passion for cooking, offering new flavors and techniques. After shifts, I'd join the pub crowd, where the bartender would generously buy me a pint. I'd chat with the wait staff, sharing my naive perspectives about life outside the U.S. while absorbing everything I could about their cultures.

My time at the Blue Ox was brief, but the impact was profound. Coming from where I did to find myself in such a place was a journey I never took for granted. I absorbed every aspect of it–the food, whisky, beer, music, and people of Limerick, Cork, Dublin, Belfast, Edinburgh, London, Amsterdam, and a quaint town called Carlisle. This trip was transformative, filled with experiences like sleeping outside a 10th-century Scottish castle, enjoying psychedelics in Amsterdam, singing Irish rebel songs on a bus in county Cork, hitchhiking hundreds of miles, sneaking into a major festival, losing my passport in an English girl's shed (wink), and spending a night outside a Somali family's home in London. The adventure was a testament to my ability to sell myself, cook, and find food, aka a little shoplifting, all essential skills that helped me survive and thrive on this epic journey. (SIDE QUEST #2 ACROSS THE POND).

Returning to the States, I was brimming with excitement and a newfound thirst for knowledge. I really wanted to refine myself, to become cultured.

Despite shedding some of my old identity—that of a poor kid with a chip on his shoulder from a rough neighborhood—I was very aware of who I was and, more importantly, who I wanted to become. My travels had been instrumental, providing me with the necessary tools to lead a fulfilling life. Similarly, my experiences in the kitchen had uniquely equipped me for successful traveling.

One of my half-sisters from my biological father's side—he had six children with three different women—was working as a server in a restaurant in Connecticut's capital city, Hartford. At that time, Hartford was a lively city, still home to the Whalers, an NHL team, and buzzing with energy. She had recently moved into an apartment in the Colt Building, the historic Colt gun factory transformed into industrial art studios. The space was too large for her alone, and given that we had only met a few years earlier after I connected with my biological father, living together seemed like a perfect opportunity to catch up on lost time. Additionally, a sauté position had opened up at her restaurant, Black-Eyed Sally's. The vibrant city life and the artistic environment of the Colt Building seemed appealing—it was the kind of culture-rich setting I was seeking. So, I thought to myself, "Let's do it."

My interview with Chef Benny left a strong first impression. He came across as smart, with a laid-back demeanor, a good sense of humor, and a hint of social awkwardness. The interview was brief—he didn't delve into too many questions, and I suspect his crush on my sister worked in my favor. As for me, I wasn't overly concerned. After all, a kitchen is a kitchen, right? Little did I know my culinary bubble was on the brink of bursting?

Upon being hired, I received a tour of the kitchen. The setup was unlike anything I'd worked with before. This was my first time being responsible for a proper line: twelve burners and two ovens under my charge. Initially, I wasn't nervous—I hadn't yet seen the line in full swing. In hindsight, I should have been bracing myself.

My first shift at Black-Eyed Sally's began with an orientation from Danny, a middle-aged cook juggling this job with another civilian role. His sense of humor and openness about his personal life, including tales of his trips to Asia and experiences with a mail-order bride, quickly broke the ice. He guided me through the preparation of dishes like jambalaya, crab cakes, and étouffée—all unfamiliar to me. Despite not knowing their ideal appearance or taste, I was thrust into the task of cooking them. I had confidently assured Chef Benny of my capabilities, and now it was time to deliver. By the end of that first week, and especially after the busy Friday shift, I thought I had a decent grasp of things, even though I was still learning.

The real test came the next day, a Saturday, known for its early start and notorious busyness. When the Hartford Whalers played at the nearby Civic Center, the restaurant buzzed with energy. I arrived to find Chef Jake, the sous chef, asking if I had prepared my prep list for the night. "No problem," I assured him, only to learn that Danny wouldn't be there to help. Chef Jake, stationed at the broiler next to me, could oversee my work, which provided some comfort. I prepped my station, got my pans ready, grabbed a pitcher of coffee and cola, and braced myself.

The first orders started rolling in at 4:01 p.m. I'll never forget that first ticket: two crab cakes, twelve oysters (on hold), one étouffée, one jambalaya, one catfish, one sirloin medium—most of which were from my station. Then, as another ticket began printing, Chef Benny shouted from the expo, "Justin, echo?" Confused, I hesitated until Chef Jake explained I needed to acknowledge hearing the order. The printer kept spewing tickets, orders kept coming, and I quickly realized I was in over my head. "I'm fucked," I thought to myself as I scrambled to cook.

In the midst of my struggle, Chef Benny called over to me. His words, "Justin, can I talk to you? Just focus. You got this," somehow snapped me out of my daze. I cooked relentlessly, barely noticing the burns I sustained in the process. I was determined to prove myself to Chef Benny and find my purpose, if only for the moment.

By the time we plated the last ticket, I felt like I had just weathered a storm at sea. Totally exhausted but filled with a newfound respect for my teammates. I thought I had also earned the respect of everyone around me. Eagerly, I awaited Chef Jake's assessment, anticipating some form of acknowledgment for my efforts. His response, however, was plainly straightforward: "You'll get it." His words, devoid of humor, carried a weight of truth. That evening, I had depleted all of my prep halfway through service, had long ticket times, and even had to redo several dishes per Chef Benny. Almost even worse, I realized my performance had impacted the servers' tips, a responsibility I hadn't fully appreciated until now. Moreover, I noticed the team heading to the upstairs bar, Pig's Eye Pub, without inviting me along.

However, in the face of these setbacks, my determination didn't waver. I understood that this was a crucial moment for learning and growth. That night, as I walked home in the cold air, the quiet around me was peaceful and so different from the chaos in the kitchen. The absence of ticket printers was a brief relief. The smell of onions and garlic clung to me, and the pain from each burn started to set in. It was a true lesson in preparedness. I awoke from a nightmare that night, haunted by the relentless sound of tickets printing from my printer.

The following shifts saw me transform into a whirlwind of preparation. Armed with a pitcher of coffee and Coca-Cola, my tongs, and my towel, I was a man on a mission. My pans were stacked and hot, and my cast irons were ready to go. I was ready, primed for the onslaught. It was then that I truly understood the essence of *mise en place*–not just as a culinary concept, but as a state of mind, a readiness for whatever the kitchen would throw at me next. You needed that to execute a plan. Just a fun note: I became so good with my towel I could actually hit a fly out of the air with a whip crack…every time.

The other team members already knew to have their shit ready. I was a double-A ball player on a major league team. Nobody in the entire restaurant was like anyone I had worked with before. The entire place was a hodgepodge of all the social differences there were: gender, sexual orientation, age, social class, religion, and ability. This was an overload of wonderful differences for me to explore and appreciate. I just sat back and got better at my job and watched. As I got better at my job, I started to gain attention from the front-of-house staff and the back-of-house staff. Eventually, I was even invited upstairs for a beer. The first to embrace me were my immediate teammates.

Chef Jake talked the most. He talked so much that it actually became a drag because all he would do was complain. About everything. Work and home. But when he went home, it actually started to get fun. The core of the team was Carlos, who was on raw bar, and Darlene on cold, aka salads.

Carlos was Peruvian and had moved to the country only a couple of years ago. He lived on Park Street, a predominantly Latino section of Hartford. His humor made my shift much more tolerable, and his talent for shucking oysters was beyond impressive. He was one of the funniest people I ever met. He also loved to laugh which brought out the childhood class clown in me. It was so easy and so fun to make him laugh. I was extremely inappropriate and he loved it. Very different times then. We were both essentially kids also. Although we were both so young, his life was very different. He had three kids and a wife. They were the hardest-working, most generous couple I have ever met in my entire life. Carlos quickly became a real friend.

Darlene was from north Hartford and brought a unique presence to our team. An African American lesbian and an army veteran, she balanced her life raising a child with her wife or "wifey" while managing her duties in the kitchen with unmatched compassion and wisdom. Functioning as our informal sergeant, Darlene kept Carlos and me in line, often with just a glance, yet she occasionally indulged in our playful antics. Meeting her wife and daughter was a revelation for me, exposing me to a family dynamic I had never considered. Their relationship, rooted in love, struck me as profoundly normal, far more so than any family structure I had previously encountered.

Our team in the kitchen had evolved into an unstoppable force, seamlessly handling every dinner rush with unflappable efficiency. I was a real line cook and that is an actual badge in our business. Black-Eyed Sally's even brought in a second sauté cook to assist me, though finding someone who could keep pace proved challenging.

This camaraderie extended beyond the kitchen, especially with the front-of-house staff, who were almost a different breed but also very much the same. Post-shift, it was a ritual for all of us to unwind upstairs at Pig's Eye Pub. Well, mostly me from the kitchen and sometimes Carlos. The bartenders, servers, and runners, flush with cash from their nightly tips, contrasted with our kitchen staff, who had to make our paychecks last. Yet, our reputation in the kitchen often earned us drinks paid for by either grateful servers or generous patrons.

Pig's Eye Pub was a unique mashup–part dive bar, part college hangout, and a haven for industry professionals. Within its walls, the restaurant industry's hierarchy was respected and revered. The establishment was a sanctuary for those in the trade, where your standing was determined not by social status but by your skill and work ethic. Meritocracy reigned supreme, making respect a valuable currency among us. Initially unfamiliar with this culture, I quickly adapted and grew to love it. The sense of achievement and recognition within this community was exhilarating.

CHAPTER FOUR

CROSSROADS AND CHOICES

At this time, I was in a long-distance relationship with a girl from Montreal whom I had met while camping in Algonquin, Maine. She had visited me in Hartford, and I had been to Montreal to visit her. After spending some time traveling through the U.K. and Northern Europe, I was thrilled to experience Montreal and be dating a girl with a Quebecois accent. She seemed very exotic, yet she was only eight hours away by train and then bus. I adored Montreal—it was everything I imagined France would be, and I was still bitten by the bug of exploration. Coming from humble beginnings, this was the start of my cultural adventure. I was sipping wine and sampling rabbit and ostrich for the first time. My Quebecoise girlfriend introduced me to the sounds of Claude Lamothe, a French-Canadian cellist who had crafted his own unique style. I was captivated.

I began writing her letters, transitioning from street urchin to romantic. My first real culinary test came at a wedding in downtown Montreal. We sat down to eat, and the first course was escargot encased in puff pastry with garlic butter. Determined to appear brave and cultured in front of my French girlfriend, I tackled the chewy, meaty morsels with gusto. Just as I was powering through, my girlfriend shrieked. "What's wrong?" I asked. She replied, "Eww, there are mushrooms in here." To me, that seemed nuts! — mushrooms never slid across the ground, leaving a slimy trail or sporting antennae. At least I had played my part; I finished the entire dish.

Eventually, we broke up—not because of the mushrooms, but because things were getting too serious. She wanted me to move to Quebec, go to school, and become a "better me." Her family was very affluent, and she was on her way to becoming a successful writer. I wasn't ready. I had much more to learn about life, and deep down, I knew it. The experience, however, opened me up in so many ways.

I learned from the restaurant rumor mill that Chef Benny had put in his notice and was planning to leave. This news hit hard – he wasn't just my mentor, he was the anchor who could steady me through the whirlwind of the busiest nights. His departure raised questions about the future of our team. Later, I discovered that Chef Benny had a pattern of short stints at restaurants. He was to be the opening chef at least seven or nine different venues in the future and I wouldn't be surprised if there were more. The irony wasn't lost on me – it seemed I shared his itch for movement. This career, as I was coming to realize, caters to those with a wandering spirit and vagabonds, something I found in myself and evidently in many others in the industry.

I was at a crossroads, contemplating my next step. Should I stay or should I go? Being a chef wasn't my ultimate goal; I was simply good at what I did and fell in love with the lifestyle it afforded me. One day, I found myself in the owner's office. He invited me to sit down for a chat about my future at the restaurant, particularly in light of Chef Benny's upcoming departure. I shared with him my appreciation for the time spent there and the bond with the team, though I admitted that I hadn't made any concrete decisions about my future, either to stay or to leave. "We've seen you as a cornerstone in that line," he said. "If you're considering staying, we'd like to increase your pay from $9 to $11 an hour." In today's terms, that was a bump from $18 to $22 an hour – a substantial offer for a 23-year-old without formal training. It was an ego boost and a significant gesture. Reflecting on it now, it was likely a strategic move to stabilize the kitchen amidst the upcoming changes. Still, it was a generous offer. The owners, with their longstanding history as restaurateurs in Hartford, clearly knew what they were doing. Their ability to maintain consistent success didn't surprise me, and this wouldn't be the last time I'd work for legendary owners in the industry.

That evening, I made my pilgrimage to Pig's Eye Pub, drinking with fellow cooks and industry folks from around town. It felt like a gathering of tribes, where everyone sported their kitchen uniforms like gang colors. It was a tight-knit community where everyone knew each other, or at least knew of each other. As the night got more and more loose-lipped, I struck up a conversation with Sully, the sous chef from Hot Tomato's, a renowned restaurant in downtown Hartford. Known for its bustling atmosphere and visually impressive open kitchen, Hot Tomato's was the cat's meow of culinary excellence. Their chefs wore pristine white coats, a symbol of their big-league reputation. But the true legend of Hartford's hospitality scene was the front of the house manager, Coop. His ability to remember every guest, his impeccable timing, and his uncanny knack for being exactly where he was needed made him more than human; he was a hospitality machine. He later became one of the owners of one of the best restaurants in Hartford County.

When Chef Sully casually mentioned he'd like to have me on their line, the idea instantly intrigued me. To be a part of such a distinguished team was an exciting prospect. "I'll arrange an interview for you with Teddy," he said. Teddy wasn't just anyone – he was a major player. His fingers were in many of Hartford's most popular college bars, and he was the owner of Hot Tomato's itself. The opportunity to interview with him was not something I could pass up. "Yes, please," I responded, already imagining the possibilities that lay ahead.

On the day of my interview, I headed to Hot Tomato's, arriving before they opened. I was escorted into the bar area where Teddy sat alongside another man. Teddy's expression read 'let's have some fun' as he greeted me.

"You're the guy Chef Sully was talking about?" he asked.

"Yep, that's me," I replied confidently.

"Can you cook?" was his straightforward response.

"I sure can," I responded.

The man beside Teddy, who stood around 6 foot 5, interjected with a surprising question. "Why work for this guy? Wouldn't you prefer to run your own kitchen? Why not come work for me instead?"

Caught off guard, I hesitated, unsure how to navigate this unexpected twist. Laughing it off seemed risky, and I wondered whether asking who he might be would come off as rude.

Thankfully, Teddy stepped in. "Justin, meet Alex. He's a partner at two great college bars in the West End."

I'd never heard of those places, but at least now I knew who he was.

Alex continued, "Seriously if you're up for it, I can offer you the Kitchen Manager. Your menu, a salary of $350 a week." That's about $693 in today's money.

Teddy, clearly irritated by this turn of events, challenged me: "Really, Alex? Right now? Okay, Justin, your call. Work for Alex, or join us here?"

Caught in their crossfire, I wished I had time to think it over. Neither had even glanced at my resumé; this felt more like a power game than an interview. My options were clear: join one of Hartford's top kitchens in a junior role and learn a ton, or take the helm at a bar I wasn't familiar with for potentially more quick money. I chose...the college bar. It seemed like an exciting challenge, but little did I know this choice would lead me down an entirely unexpected path.

Teddy seemed unfazed by my decision. He shrugged and quipped, "At least you're staying in the family," revealing his part-ownership in the college bar.

I had the opportunity to meet Teddy several more times after our initial encounter. He epitomized the true essence of a restaurant guy. About a year later, I was invited to his riverside condo, a stunning place with views overlooking the Connecticut River. Perched high above, the vantage point offered a unique perspective where the fireworks seemed to burst at eye level. Teddy's annual 4th of July party was an epic event attended by selected staff and other industry professionals. It underscored my progress and standing in the hospitality world, an honor that wasn't lost on me. Or it could have been that I was in the right place at the right time; either way, I was there. His hospitality was as expansive as his view – incredibly generous and always memorable.

Teddy's untimely passing in 2005 left a profound impact on the industry and on me personally. He was only 44 at the time, five years younger than I am as I write this book. I was just 23 during our memorable interview. The words that rippled through the culinary world suggested that he had taken his own life, a revelation that was both shocking and deeply saddening, if at all true.

Teddy's success and admiration within our community made it hard to comprehend the struggles he must have faced behind the scenes. This tragic event underscored a harsh reality that I've come to recognize in our industry: mental health challenges, including depression, addiction, and the risk of suicide, are often hidden beneath the surface of even the most seemingly successful individuals.

While there's much I didn't know about Teddy's personal struggles and much I may never understand, his passing was a sobering reminder of the importance of mental health awareness and support in our industry. It was not the first, nor would it be the last time. And when I was in the scene, I'd encounter these issues so closely intertwined with the high-pressure environment of hospitality life.

I gave my notice at Black-Eyed Sally's and started at the college bar very soon after. The bar was nestled in a unique neighborhood – an eclectic mix of bohemian artistry, worn-down residential blocks, and college housing. This diverse and vibrant area presented a completely different atmosphere; I was no longer downtown.

During this time, I also moved out of my sister's artist loft, opting to live with my long-time friend Paul, whom I traveled Europe with, to a grittier part of Hartford. The location was conveniently walkable to work, yet it was also far enough that my daily commute often involved navigating through a gauntlet of tempting offers – from "good time" companionship to various drugs. Despite the surroundings, I never faced any serious troubles. My experiences had taught me valuable lessons: the importance of respect given is respect gained, the art of minding my own business, and I already knew to never get swindled again.

My first day at the college bar was a real eye-opener. As I stepped into the kitchen, I couldn't help but question my decision: "What the hell did I sign up for?" The floor was uneven, littered with paint, chips, and holes. The setup was basic: a 5-foot hood covering a 4-burner oven, a flat top, and a salamander, accompanied by a 2-door sandwich prep cooler and a 3-bay sink. I met my first coworker, Ross, known as Round Ross. He was chatting with some distinctive-looking bar guests as I approached. Hailing from New York City, he was eager to have some quality food in the place. The bar's atmosphere revealed it as a college and neighborhood haunt. Time to get cooking.

Truth be told, I wasn't prepared for this challenge, though I didn't realize it then. I hired my friend Paul as a dishwasher and prep cook. Despite having zero cooking experience, not needing a job, and being perpetually high, he was on board. It was a rocky start. Post-shift, I discovered the bar's vibrant nightlife. It was a hub for students from the University of Hartford and Trinity College, tons of life with a DJ playing loud and great music and a palpable sense of debauchery.

The bar team was in its element, tirelessly serving an array of drinks – Red Bull and Jäger, tequila shots, Jack and Cokes. The lead bartender, Ricky, was suave, tan, with spiked hair, a big grin, tattoos, and a shell necklace. He just pointed at me, "NEW COOK!" before serving up a generously poured Jack and Coke on the house. This reciprocation of favors was a common practice among us.

The team was legendary in their own right – rock gods in the eyes of their admirers. I met Skip, the aspiring pharmacist; the other Ross, aka the Love Muscle; Messy, soon to be Hartford's first known mixologist; Tammy, the only girl; and Bill, a name later to become well-known. Even the bouncers had a demi-god status in this realm. At that moment, I felt a powerful draw towards this lifestyle. It fit like a glove and I wanted to be one of them.

Across the street was our sister bar, the college bar II, notorious for its fake IDs and frequent raids. Summarizing my time at the college bar, I admit I gave in to the temptations. Drugs of all kinds were rampant, drinking a daily ritual, and promiscuity the norm – it was like living the backstage life of a rock concert every night. One of my favorite nights was when myself, round Ross, Kyle the bouncer, and three girls who made it past last call, closed up the bar and at 3ish in the a.m. decided to play strip golden tee video golf, which Round Ross and I would always play during the slow times. It was a good game to win.

A particularly low moment came with a young, newish bartender from the college bar II, whom I didn't exactly like. He was a rich kid and I still had a chip on my shoulder. He ordered a burger from us and instead of the delicious burger, I sent over a dead pigeon in a to-go container to him. It was an act I sort of regret and considered the lowest point of my culinary journey and yet, still think it's funny. Despite the chaos and my actions, I look back at this chapter as a crucial period of learning and I am grateful to have survived it. My rough childhood and wild days in Amsterdam were other times I narrowly escaped serious consequences.

Reflecting on those days, I realize how much I've grown from the person I was then. While I may not be proud of everything I did at the college bar, it taught me invaluable lessons about the world of high-volume college bars, the dangers of excess, and the importance of making better choices. This chapter of my life, filled with recklessness and learning, was a pivotal point in shaping the person I am today. It's a reminder of where I've been and how far I've come. If I'm being honest, it was also pretty fun.

My time at the college bar was relatively short-lived. Alex had high expectations, and I soon realized I wasn't the right fit for what he envisioned. Moreover, the bar itself wasn't quite prepared for his ambitious plans. However, Alex's dream did eventually materialize. He went on to open a successful burger and bourbon bar, with several locations now in operation. Bill, the bartender I mentioned earlier, also carved out his success with his own restaurant group, an American-style pub and grill restaurant that has expanded to ten locations. As for Love Muscle Ross, he partnered with Skip to open a downtown bar, which, while short-lived, was a bold attempt. Messy gained renown as a bartender, even shaking at the Oscars and becoming a sake expert. Tammy, as far as I know, settled into married life and now works at an insurance company. Suave's whereabouts are uncertain, but rumors suggest that he's living a leisurely life by the pool or beach. Almost everyone I worked with at the college bar went on to have successful careers in the hospitality industry.

After the college bar, my journey led me to various unusual gigs. I worked in the breakfast cafeteria of a corporate office building for a few months and even took a stint cooking at a strip club. Contrary to what one might expect, the kitchen there was surprisingly well-maintained and clean. I was the opening cook at a barbecue place in the middle of nowhere Connecticut for a guy who had no idea about restaurants but had a good barbeque sauce recipe. According to him, he made it with coffee cola which I found interesting but again, no idea about the business. We had three customers a day. My days in the kitchen were drawing to a close.

During this period, Paul, my former roommate and a constant collaborator in our movie-making dreams, had moved to the Bronx in New York City. He was learning the filmmaking craft and had taken over his grandmother's rent-controlled apartment. He suggested I join him there. After all, movies were made in New York, not Hartford. At that point, I felt stuck in a rut and needed a change. So, at 25, I cut my long hair, sold all my belongings, and made a move to the Bronx, ready to embark on a new chapter and chase those big-screen dreams.

CHAPTER FIVE

FROM CITY TO CITY TO CITY

Back to New York City I went, finding it transformed from the place I remembered seven years earlier. My career path might have been entirely different had I accepted the position at Hot Tomato's. Perhaps I would have been a sous chef by now, still immersed in the culinary world. However, witnessing the dynamic energy of the bar team at the college bar, a desire for change ignited in me. It was this restlessness, this yearning for something beyond the kitchen, that propelled me toward a new direction. NYC might be the perfect place to start that journey.

Paul had a one-month head start on me in New York. By the time I arrived, he had already acclimated himself, exploring the city and engaging with a variety of people. He had this unique ability, somewhat reminiscent of Forrest Gump, where his straightforward and unassuming manner often led him into extraordinary situations and conversations, sometimes with people who were seemingly out of our league.

When I arrived, Paul was there to greet me at Grand Central Station. We plunged into the subway's hustle and bustle, a sensory overload compared to what I was used to. At the subway map, Paul began to explain the system to me. "We need the green line, the 4-5-6 trains. Remember, the 4 and 5 are express," he said. I stared at the map, bewildered, not understanding a word. But it didn't take long for me to get the hang of it, and soon, I was navigating the complex train schedules of New York City like a pro. It was just the beginning of a much larger learning curve and a series of adventures awaiting me in this awesome city.

When Paul and I realized we needed jobs, we stumbled upon a wedding venue in the East Tremont neighborhood of the Bronx, the Marina Del Rey. Intrigued, we applied and, to our surprise, both landed positions as banquet waiters. Our experience in this field was non-existent, but that didn't seem to matter. The only requirement was owning a cheap tuxedo, and conveniently, they directed us to a place where we could get outfitted. The job paid a modest $60 per shift, but the venue itself was stunning – a family-owned gem right on the East River.

It was my first experience as a waiter. The other members of the facility were young kids, college dropouts, adults who had exhausted other options and all were locals. Not for nutin' but the accents were lovely. The venue hosted events of all kinds – weddings across different faiths and cultures, bat mitzvahs, bereavements, and reunions. Each event was a new cultural experience, enriching in ways I hadn't anticipated.

The antics at the wedding venue were wild and endlessly entertaining. Unsupervised, people would indulge in all sorts of mischief – from sneaking drinks and eating from guests' plates to fraternizing in the venue's hidden corners. On occasion, someone straight out of a Martin Scorsese movie would slip us a twenty or so. Most of the tips, however, ended up with the valet, bar staff, and captains, who sometimes shared their spoils. It was an okay job, but not quite what I had in mind when I moved to NYC. I wasn't looking to ride public buses in a cheap tux through the Bronx; I wanted to reinvent myself, and Manhattan seemed like the right place for that.

I had a bit of acting experience, having starred in an indie gangster film back in Hartford, which had made it to video stores like Blockbuster and Hollywood Video, pre-streaming era. Coincidentally, the director of that film was now in NYC and tipped me off about a production assistant position on a Lower East Side movie set for *The Hours* starring Meryl Streep, Ed Harris, and Nicole Kidman. Following his lead, I landed the job, which paid $150 a day – a significant step up from my previous gig.

Working for Paramount, my tasks included managing sidewalk traffic (a thankless job where New Yorkers often told me exactly where to go), fetching coffee for the director, and relaying messages. Despite the occasional challenge, it was cool to see stars like Meryl Streep in action and to be part of a real film crew.

After *The Hours* wrapped, Paul and I dove into our own creative project. We wrote and filmed a movie on 16mm in our neighborhood, balancing this with our jobs at the wedding venue. The film wasn't great, but we were living out our dream. During this time, Paul became friends with a chef from a Pervuian restauraunt on 83rd and Amsterdam in Manhattan called Sipan. We all went out one night for cocktails and I was inspired to try bartending in Manhattan and I was going to bring it up to her. However, my previous interview experience for a serving position in the Lower East Side lingered in my mind as a stark reality check.

In that interview, I found myself among over thirty candidates, clutching a resumé that was far from impressive and then I was bewildered by the request for a headshot – a requirement I still can't quite grasp. When my turn arrived, it was evident to the managers that I wasn't the ideal candidate, yet they courteously proceeded with the interview. The moment they dove into wine knowledge, I was unmistakably out of my element. It was a clear signal that I wasn't suited for the role, and I exited the interview fully aware of the vast scope of knowledge I needed to acquire. The sting of embarrassment that day served as a major motivator for me.

After enjoying a few drinks and building a friendly rapport with Chef Natalia, the Argentinean chef at Sipan, I decided to inquire about a bartending position. She informed me they weren't looking for bartenders but might have an opening for a server.

"Do you have any serving experience?" she asked.

"Yes, I'm currently a server at a fantastic venue," I replied, embellishing my experience a bit.

Natalia seemed convinced and offered me the chance to start the following week. And just like that, Manhattan became my new stage.

When I arrived for my first shift at the restaurant, I was instantly plunged into a whole new world of learning. I quickly realized that catering service and restaurant service were worlds apart, especially in a high-end establishment like this one. My previous experience didn't prepare me for the nuances of this upscale environment. Firstly, there was no formal clock-in system. The first five shifts were essentially a trial period and unpaid. In the competitive world of Manhattan's dining scene, it seemed training was a privilege, not a compensated necessity.

The venue was very charming with understated elegance. Each table was adorned with wine glasses and draped in tablecloths, creating a warm and inviting atmosphere. Candles placed at the center meant to cast a glow on the neatly arranged plates and silverware, including the ever-important salad fork. As I checked out the room, I couldn't help but wonder about the new challenge I had stepped into.

My guide through this new world was Jose, a 30-year-old Ecuadorian who lived in Queens. He greeted me warmly, mentioning that Chef Natalia had spoken highly of me. My early lessons in socializing and drinking, honed from a young age, now seemed particularly useful in making a good impression on a seasoned chef. "Let's get to work," he said, his tone a blend of friendliness and professionalism.

He started my training with the basics of glass polishing. As he handed me a cloth, he emphasized the crucial role of immaculate wine glasses in our service.

"Our goal is to sell a bottle of wine as soon as possible. If we don't sell a bottle, we clear the glasses away," he explained.

"Sounds shameful," I commented, attempting to inject some humor into the learning process.

"It is," he said, sharing a conspiratorial grin that instantly put me at ease.

Then, he meticulously demonstrated the table setting protocol: the dinner plate centered, flanked by the dinner fork on the left and the salad fork just beside it. To the right lay the knife and spoon, with the water glass strategically placed above and to the right of the plate. A neatly folded cloth napkin, shaped into an elegant triangle, rested in the center of each plate.

"What's next?" I inquired, eager to learn more.

"We set up for the family meal," he replied, signaling the start of our next task.

Family meal was a concept entirely new to me, yet it instantly captivated my heart. Jose and I prepared a large table to accommodate about 10-12 people, complete with plates, silverware, pitchers of water, and napkins. Soon, kitchen staff began to arrive, one bearing a hotel pan brimming with beef, followed by others with french fries or *papas fritas*, and rice and tomatoes. Everyone paused their prep and side work to gather around the table. Chef Natalia took her place at the head, signaling the start of the meal. As we enjoyed the food, I was introduced to Luis, the seasoned dishwasher from Guatemala, and Sixto from Ecuador. Sixto, in particular, caught my attention with his infectious humor, chubby cheeks and toothless smile, and unique bowl cut. His cheerful nature was truly infectious.

The meal itself was a revelation. Chef Natalia explained we were enjoying *lomo saltado*, a staple from the menu. This traditional Peruvian stir-fry, blending marinated sirloin strips with onions, tomatoes, and french fries, served over rice, was a delightful fusion from the Chifa tradition, where Chinese cuisine meets Peruvian flavors. The dish, now a mainstream cultural staple, was a delicious eye-opener for me.

Eventually, I sampled more menu items like *arroz con pato, causa,* and *ceviche,* and my culinary horizons expanded exponentially. Moving to New York proved to be as crucial to my culinary education as my travels to the U.K. There, I learned about lamb burgers, Yorkshire pudding, and rashers. Here in Manhattan and the Bronx, I encountered a world of flavors just as foreign and exciting, even though I was back in my home country.

Quickly, I discovered that even ordering a pizza could be an adventure. Our local pizzeria, Emilio's at the corner of Haight Avenue and Williamsbridge, was one of many in the neighborhood, each boasting the title of "the best." One day, eager for a taste of pizza, I decided to order what I thought was a simple pizza. I called up Emilio's and confidently requested, "I'd like a large hamburger and pepperoni, please."

There was a pause on the other end before the puzzled reply came, "Hamburg? You mean meat sauce?'

"No, hamburger," I clarified.

"Meatballs?" he asked, still confused.

I was getting nowhere. "No, you know, like ground hamburger meat."

The frustration was evident in his voice as he responded, "I don't understand what you want. Are you sure you don't mean meat sauce?"

It dawned on me then he had no idea what I was talking about. I sighed, realizing the cultural gap in pizza toppings here.

"Meatball is fine," I conceded, accepting the local pizza vocabulary.

Discovering that ground hamburger wasn't common here, and a "grinder" was actually called a "hero," was part of adapting to New York life. It turned out the pizza at Emilio's, despite the topping confusion, was the best I'd ever had.

I soon learned that the Bronx was a haven for fantastic comfort food, while Manhattan's restaurants were invariably top-notch – if they weren't, they wouldn't last a week. I found that nothing beat a 75-cent coffee from a street cart, every bagel was a delight, and the best egg sandwiches were found in bodegas.

I became a master of the subway system, familiarizing myself with the neighborhoods and their bars. However, despite this newfound city savvy, I was still green as a server.

My first night on the job, after completing my training, was a real test. The first two tables went smoothly, but then came a six-top, all the women in fur coats. I sensed this was a well-to-do crowd. They were regulars, enthusiastic about their favorite restaurant. They ordered wine – two Malbecs, two Chardonnays, a Sauvignon Blanc, and a Cabernet Sauvignon. I was lost in the unfamiliar names but scribbled them down anyway.

When the bar prepared the wines, they were placed on a tray. I contemplated making three trips instead of using a tray. The bartender laughed off my suggestion, thinking it was a joke.

Slowly, I managed to deliver four glasses without incident. But as I reached for the fifth, the tray tipped, spilling Sauvignon Blanc all over a guest's fur coat. To my surprise, everyone at the table burst into laughter.

"I'm so sorry!" I exclaimed.

"It's fine, you already put down all the reds," a guest reassured me.

I thought my job was over then and there. I informed the bartender and Chef Natalia about the mishap and quickly returned with a replacement glass, trying to lighten the mood with a joke about spilling again. To my relief, they all laughed. A big gamble but I was too naive to know better.

Chef Natalia later reassured me that the guests liked me despite the accident. That table left me a $60 tip. I realized then that the confidence and charm I'd honed selling perfume could work wonders, even in moments of crisis. But how long could I keep up this facade? Sadly, not much longer.

That morning began like any other until a phone call jolted me awake. It was 2001, and cell phones weren't as ubiquitous as they are now, so the landline ringing was my only alert.

"Hello?" I mumbled, still groggy.

"Hey man," came Damien's voice, a known prankster in our group. "Did you see what happened?"

"What? What time is it?" I asked, confused.

"A plane just crashed into a building in New York," he blurted out.

"A small plane, like a Cessna?" I asked, skeptical of his antics.

"No, a jet. A big one." His tone was serious, a rarity for him.

Dismissing it as another of his pranks, I hung up. But barely half an hour later, the phone rang again.

"Another plane hit the other Trade Center building," Damien's voice was frantic this time.

I was now fully alert. "What? When?"

"Just now. Turn on the TV."

I flicked on the TV, but all I got was static. No channels were coming through, a bizarre occurrence since we always received basic channels even without cable.

"I'll call you back," I said, switching to the radio.

The radio confirmed it: a second plane had hit the South Tower. "This is an attack," the broadcaster announced. "Additional planes may be at risk."

"Holy shit," I muttered, the gravity of the situation sinking in.

I barged into Paul's room. "Wake up, something crazy's happening!"

"Get out, I'm sleeping," he mumbled, uninterested.

In disbelief, I returned to the radio. News of the Pentagon and a downed plane in Pennsylvania came through. Our landline went dead. I burst into Paul's room again.

"We are at war!" I exclaimed, but he remained unresponsive.

The radio reported bomb scares at the Capitol. The Twin Towers were ablaze. I rushed to the roof and gazed towards the southern skyline and it was engulfed in smoke; both towers were visibly damaged.

Feeling disconnected from the world with no phone or TV, I ran to the neighborhood store and bought a disposable camera, driven by an unexplainable urge to document the moment.

Back on the roof, Moira, the Irish superintendent, joined me. We both stared in shock and silence, neither of us having more information.

As I watched, the North Tower collapsed into a cloud of smoke and debris, quickly followed by the South Tower. It was surreal, watching them fall right before my eyes.

All those people. "What the fuck is happening?" I thought.

The roar of F-16 fighter jets overhead snapped me out of my trance. At that moment, I made a decision that would alter my life's trajectory: I needed to join the army. I needed to play a part to gain some control in this new, changed world.

Life in New York City had come to a standstill. Eventually, our TV and phone services resumed, but the city was in a state of suspended animation, everyone trying to comprehend the new reality. The subway stations were teeming with people from all walks of life, some rushing to Ground Zero to help, others simply glued to their TVs, anxiously awaiting updates.

I had to act and I found myself walking into a recruitment office. "I want to join," I declared to the soldier on duty.

"Let's get started," he replied efficiently.

I filled out the necessary paperwork and scheduled tests. Aware of friends who'd been misled into less-than-desirable army roles, I was determined to carve my own path. My goal was clear: I wanted a role in journalism, with the 46R Military Occupational Specialty if I remember correctly. I knew it might still involve combat duty as I was informed, but I was ready.

The physical examination began smoothly. I discreetly omitted to mention my asthma, and everything else seemed fine until the hearing test. My left ear has 80% hearing loss, which I didn't think would be a significant issue until I failed the initial test.

An officer came into the room, concerned. "Are the headphones working correctly?"

He checked the connections and then, with an understanding nod, I confessed, "I have hearing difficulties in my left ear."

"No problem, let's try this again," he assured me.

As we restarted the test, I could hear the beeps in my right ear without any issue. Whenever a beep sounded in my left ear, I noticed an officer on the other side of the glass subtly raising his finger. Taking his cue, I raised my left hand each time. With this improvised system, I miraculously passed the second test with "flying colors."

After a few more straightforward tests, I was all set. Interestingly, I was informed that my test results qualified me for a broader range of positions than the one I initially applied for. They even offered substantial signing bonuses of up to 15 thousand dollars for other roles. However, this decision wasn't about money for me. I was steadfast in my choice and we finalized the assignment. I signed the paperwork, though there was one more step – getting my tattoos approved by a higher-ranking officer.

A recruiting officer drove me to my potential base in Brooklyn for this final check. My tattoos were inspected and deemed acceptable, clearing me to join the ranks and take my oath. In a room with about six other recruits, a sense of excitement filled the air. A ranking officer instructed us to raise our right hands and repeat after him. We did so, each of us undoubtedly feeling a deep sense of pride. I was ready, or I thought I was.

Returning home, I knew I had about a month before shipping off to Fort Jackson for basic training. I gave notice at my jobs, sold whatever I couldn't save, and made all the necessary farewells.

In the meantime, my job at Marina Del Rey kept me preoccupied. We hosted numerous bereavement services for local firefighters in the aftermath of the recent tragic events, often several in a single day. The Marina Del Rey, once boasting a view of the iconic Twin Towers, now faced a skyline forever altered. The reality of it all had set in; I was prepared for my next chapter.

However, about two weeks after finalizing everything with the army, I received an unexpected phone call.

"Hello, this is Lieutenant so and so," the voice on the other end said. "It appears that there's been a falsification on your army application."

Confused, I responded, "Huh? What do you mean?"

"The application lists you as having a driver's license, a requirement for the 46r Military Occupational Specialty you applied for. Do you have a driver's license?"

I replied truthfully, "I do not. But I never claimed to have one."

"Well, it's on your application. Unfortunately, we cannot process your enlistment, and you'll be barred from reapplying for a certain period. This is now an ongoing investigation."

I was in disbelief; I gave the oath, almost thinking it was a prank. To be fair, maybe I completely misunderstood the conversation I had with this lieutenant. I mean, it sounded like I was in big trouble for falsifying government records or something. Looking back on it, it must have been a major misunderstanding. Maybe it was my diploma? I had my GED. Or, it seemed the recruiter might have checked off certain qualifications to expedite my acceptance. Suddenly, I found myself without a job, without plans, and no longer joining the army. Staying in NYC was no longer a viable option, yet returning to Connecticut was the last thing I wanted. I was at a crossroads, unsure of my next move.

In a state of confusion, I reached out to everyone I could think of, trying to make sense of my situation. My thoughts turned to my sister, April, with whom I had previously lived in Hartford. She had since moved to Phoenix, Arizona. I hesitated, wondering if she'd be open to the idea of me joining her there. To my relief, she was willing to give it a shot.

Inspired to make a fresh start, I contacted an old friend from Connecticut, Dave. Unlike me, he hadn't traveled much. April and Dave had previously gotten along well, so I managed to persuade him to embark on this new adventure with me. We decided to give the desert a try.

Our arrival in Phoenix was a shock to the system. The moment we stepped out of the airport, we were engulfed by a wall of heat – a staggering 115 degrees. It was a dry heat, they say, but then again, so are most ovens.

The Southwest's unique ambiance was realized in Phoenix. The landscape was dominated by shades of brown, punctuated by the occasional green cacti – exactly as one might imagine. And, of course, it was relentlessly hot.

Eager to work, I wasted no time in job hunting. With my recent experience as a server, I set my sights on similar positions, unwilling to settle for less. Despite my efforts, responses were scarce. Finally, I landed an interview at JB's on Northern Avenue – a place that, for all intents and purposes, was a less trendy version of Denny's. Despite an odd sense of entitlement, considering my limited experience as a server, I quickly realized JB's was the ideal setting for a beginner like me. The food was mediocre, the staff operated on autopilot, and the customers' expectations were low. This unremarkable eatery was the perfect training ground for me to hone my serving skills.

During my time working at JB's, I took every opportunity to explore the area with my sister and Dave. Arizona was a landscape of extremes – daily wildfires surrounded us, and the temperature seldom dipped below 110 degrees. Yet, amidst this intense heat, we found some respite. Our day trips to the stunning red rock vistas of Sedona and our nocturnal adventures in Scottsdale offered a welcome change of scenery. The culinary delights of the region were a revelation, especially the Mexican fusion cuisine. I grew up on hearty Canadian breakfasts in New England and I am now savoring the likes of *huevos rancheros*, breakfast burritos, and avocado toast – these quickly became my new favorites.

Arizona played a part in discovering my roots and was an enlightening experience. I met April shortly after reconnecting with my biological father when I was 18 – a timely re-entry into my life on his part. I learned that my father had six children with three different women. Meeting my siblings was incredible; it was a gathering of family members who actually resembled each other! My father passed away from pancreatic cancer seven years later. Ironically, I think I learned more about him after the fact than while he was alive. He had a keen interest in genealogy, believing our lineage included Native American ancestry. Initially, I was skeptical, but a DNA test confirmed his beliefs. There were traces of indigenous heritage from eastern Mexico, South Texas, Panama, and Costa Rica. Further genealogical research traced that part of our family back to the 1700s in Mexico. My time in the Southwest turned out to be a crucial step in my journey of self-discovery and understanding my heritage.

Despite these experiences, my job felt unfulfilling; it was merely a means to an end, and I quickly picked up the basics of being a server. Dave, battling homesickness and missing his girlfriend, was eager to return to Connecticut. April, too, seemed ready for us to leave her one-bedroom apartment. I

found myself missing an ex back in Connecticut and longing for family connections. With the state besieged by wildfires and dust storms, and my own personal ties pulling me back, it felt like the right time to head north again.

Back to Connecticut we went.

CHAPTER SIX

LOST AND FOUND

Coming back to Connecticut was a confusing time for me. I was 27, I had no license, I had been out of the scene for some time and when I was, I had turned into a journeyman. It was far enough from my former trajectory that it would take a lot of work to get back. I looked around for work at all the old spots to get some money in my pocket. There was nothing. Tumbleweeds. The gap from my previous career path seemed vast, and I knew it would require considerable effort to bridge it. In need of immediate income, I scoured my old haunts for work, but to my dismay, opportunities were scarce, almost non-existent. It felt like I was chasing squirrels.

In a move that felt like a regression, I moved back in with my mother and stepfather in Manchester. Seeking some semblance of familiarity, I visited Nullis Italia, one of my former culinary stomping grounds. There, I learned that Fred Anulli, the original owner, had passed away, and his son Matt had reluctantly assumed control. Matt, who seemed more invested in his music and perhaps his engineering background, was running the family business more out of obligation than passion. Despite this, he recognized me from my past tenure and informed me that there were no openings for servers or cooks, the roles I had come to identify with. However, he did offer me a part-time position as a dishwasher. I paused, considering the offer for a brief 20 seconds before accepting it. Work was work, and survival had always been my mantra, especially during the rough patches of my upbringing. If you asked me what I did, I would have said, "Whatever it takes" So, there I was at 27 – back under my mother's roof, sharing space with my stepfather and little sister, and working as a dishwasher without a driver's license. From an outside perspective, this could have been the beginning of a downward spiral.

Walking to work, a 2.5-mile journey taking almost an hour each way, wasn't entirely foreign to me. However, doing so in the town where I grew up added a layer of reflection to my daily treks. I'm sure people I knew drove by and were not surprised at my situation. This period of my life, although I initially saw it as a rise, served to humble me deeply. I wanted more than what my current situation offered. Living with my stepfather required a level of restraint I struggled to maintain, and cohabitating with my mother, who was succumbing to her addiction and poor health choices, was equally challenging. I often found myself in a reversed role, urging her to drink water and cut down on her twelve-pack-a-day soda habit, more like a concerned parent than her son. My love for her was immense, but it was hard for me to see that she might not have held the same love for herself.

Craving more work and income, I secured a job at a pizza place a few towns over, about four miles away. This meant an hour-and-a-half walk each way, a commitment I preferred over the uncertainty and waiting involved with bus travel. Now, I was working more, a small yet significant step, but I knew I needed a strategic plan for growth.

During this time, my bed was the couch in the living room of my mother's house. One night, disrupted from my sleep, my mother stood over me with an urgent request. My stepfather, who had a pattern of leaving and rarely returning, was absent at that time. "I need you to drive me to the hospital," she said softly.

Concerned, I asked, "Are you okay? What's going on?" Her previous hospital visits and stints in rehab had somewhat prepared me for such situations, but the urgency at 2 a.m. was jarring, especially since she knew I didn't have a driver's license.

"I'm not feeling great and need to get checked out," she replied with a hint of calmness.

Groggily, I put on shoes over my pajamas and we got into the car. Upon reaching the Manchester Hospital's emergency room, I offered to park and accompany her inside.

"No, go back home. Nicole is there alone," she insisted.

"Are you sure?" I asked, hesitant to leave her alone.

"Yes, I'll call when I'm ready to be picked up," she reassured me.

With a mutual exchange of "I love you," a hug, and a kiss, she stepped out and disappeared through the sliding doors of the emergency room.

Little did I know, that would be the last time I saw my mother conscious.

The next day, a call from the hospital sent a wave of anxiety through me. The doctor on the line initially inquired about my stepfather, but upon learning of his absence, they addressed me directly, advising me to come to the hospital to discuss my mother's condition. I contacted my stepfather's family to relay the message and then reached out to my aunt. Together, we headed to the hospital, where we were informed that my mother had been placed in an induced coma due to a severe case of meningitis.

The following days were a blur, a mix of routine and anxious waiting. My stepfather picked up my little sister, leaving me alone in the apartment, juggling work and daily calls to the hospital for updates. This wasn't entirely new to me; my mother's health had always been a source of worry, stemming from her stints in rehab and a previous suicide attempt when I was 16. Despite the challenges, she had always managed to pull through, which gave me a sliver of hope.

A few nights later, a call from the doctor brought a mix of relief and despair. "Good news and bad news," he began. "Your mother's condition was improving, but during the process of bringing her out of the coma, she suffered a stroke." At the hospital, my aunt and I were ushered into a private room where the doctor explained the grave situation. My mother was now on life support, showing no brain activity. The decision on whether to continue life support was now in my hands.

I remember feeling a deep sense of anger and helplessness as I sat by her bedside, holding her hand, lost in thought. The uncertainty was overwhelming; I didn't know what to do, except for the deep-seated wish to see her wake up. In that moment of contemplation, Louis Armstrong's "What a Wonderful World" softly played on a radio above her bed, such an ironic soundtrack to the situation.

That night, haunted with grief and uncertainty, I found relief in alcohol, trying to numb the pain. The next day, hungover drunk at the same time, I met with the girl I was seeing at the time for breakfast, pouring out my heart about the decision I had to make. As I spoke, "What a Wonderful World" began playing in the diner, striking a chord deep within me. It was then that I realized my mother, who had battled addiction, abuse, and the struggles of becoming a mother at 16, was ready for peace – a peace she so rightfully deserved.

Reluctantly, I made an impossible decision to let her go, a choice that shattered my heart but was, in my eyes, a final act of love and mercy for her. I informed the doctor of my decision. My stepfather was absent, leaving me to face this alone.

On the day they withdrew life support, I sat by her side, holding her hand. Her breaths, initially frequent, gradually slowed, each one drawing her closer to the end. As I felt her take her last breath, a profound sense of her spirit leaving her body enveloped me. She was gone, leaving me with memories and love that would never fade.

Death was not a stranger to me. I had experienced it before with my biological father's passing from pancreatic cancer, waking up to find my grandmother deceased when I was 10, and being present during my ex-girlfriend's father's last moments. Each experience left its mark, shaping my understanding of life's fragility and the importance of cherishing every moment we have.

I found myself unable to properly grieve for my mother. It was perplexing, this inability to process my emotions. Her funeral arrangements were modest – a wake and bereavement, as she was to be cremated. We couldn't afford anything more elaborate.

The night of the wake was emotionally charged. My younger sister, just 12 years old, delivered a remarkable eulogy. She was composed and articulate, a stark contrast to the turmoil she must have felt inside. When it was my turn to speak, I found myself overwhelmed with emotion, barely able to articulate my feelings through the tears.

The wake's somber mood gave way to a makeshift gathering in the parking lot of a church, where we drank and shared memories. After checking out what we were up to, drinking in a parking lot, the local police officers were understanding and kind, allowing us to grieve in our own way. They even offered condolences. The night culminated in a heartfelt gathering at a classic dive bar, complete with a good jukebox, where we found solace in each other's company.

In the wake of my mother's passing, I was forced to confront the reality of my situation. Her apartment was no longer an option for me. Relocating to the boonies to live with my Aunt Linda and Uncle Bruce became my only real option. Conveniently, sort of, Linda's commute passed through Manchester, offering me a ride — though it meant starting my day at six in the morning. This change meant I could no longer work at the Vernon Pizza spot, but my dishwashing job was still available, I just had to pass three hours.

A few years prior, while working on the set of *King Midas*, a film I had a starring role in, I met one of the production crew who was also a waiter at City Steam Brewery in downtown Hartford. This restaurant had evolved from the legendary Brown Thomson and Company, a renowned Hartford bar and restaurant.

In 1983, The New York Times described it as follows: "Some restaurants are for dining, others for socializing. Brown Thomson & Company in downtown Hartford excels in the latter, though it's also a visual treat. Located in a historic building designed by H. H. Richardson in 1877, it was once Connecticut's largest department store. Now a bustling restaurant, its charm lies in its unique interior. Four levels, some just alcoves with booths and tables, are adorned with brick walls, pressed-tin ceilings, Romanesque arches, and original paneling. The top level features ceiling fans driven by an intricate pulley system. Decorated with stuffed bears, bison heads, elk horns, and stained glass, it's the perfect spot for a casual meal or snack, especially after events at the nearby Hartford Civic Center or Hartford Stage Company."

The waiter, Jeff, had gotten me an interview for a serving position. This historical and architecturally rich venue was now City Steam Brewery, an establishment that preserved its legacy while introducing a modern twist. As I contemplated my next steps, the idea of working in such a storied place held a certain appeal. It was time for a new chapter, one that would hopefully bring stability and a fresh start.

On the day of the interview, I was greeted by K2, the General Manager, whose approach was a blend of lively enthusiasm and straightforward honesty. She brought a brisk energy that set the tone for our conversation.

"What position are you interviewing for again?" she asked.

"A server position," I replied confidently. "Jeff referred me."

Our conversation was brief but engaging. I emphasized my "extensive" serving experience in NYC and Phoenix, conveniently omitting my current stint as a dishwasher. I recalled a conversation with Chef Benny from Black-Eyed Sally's, where he had mentioned his girlfriend K2 from City Steam. Seizing the moment, I dropped his name, thinking it might work in my favor. Little did I know, they were no longer together, and their split hadn't been amicable. Nevertheless, I've never been one to shy away from taking a chance.

The interview progressed smoothly, and despite the unmentioned complexities surrounding Benny's name, I was offered the job. It felt like a stroke of luck, a testament to my willingness to leap into new opportunities, even when the full picture wasn't clear. I was ready to step into this new role, hopeful for what lay ahead in this iconic establishment. Only problem was, how the hell was I going to get here?

CHAPTER SEVEN

BEHIND THE BAR

Adapting to my new reality, I landed a serving job in Hartford. It was a fresh start, but it came with its own set of logistical challenges. My routine now involved catching a ride with my aunt to Manchester at 6 a.m. and hanging out until 9 a.m. for my dishwashing shift. From there, depending on my schedule, I either headed straight to Nullis or took a bus to Hartford for my serving job. To make this work, I joined a gym conveniently located a few miles from Nullis and on a bus route to Hartford. My mornings began early with a workout and a shower at the gym, providing a necessary boost for the long day ahead. On days with double shifts, a friend in Hartford graciously offered a place to crash. This juggling act of work and commute was tricky but necessary. I was determined to make the most of this serving opportunity, and I had to make this work.

Adapting to my role at City Steam demanded quick adjustment, particularly after my previous position at a venue that was akin to a Denny's in its operations. The layout of City Steam was complex: the kitchen perched on the third floor, with the comedy club nestled in the basement, making the establishment feel like the restaurant equivalent of a cruise ship—vast like the Titanic and just as sinkable on a full night. The venue was a behemoth, featuring pool tables in a back room, four bars, five restrooms, a banquet room, and several server stations scattered throughout. This expansive setup required a keen sense of orientation and efficiency, especially during peak hours.

At City Steam, professionalism was required, evident in our strict uniform checks before each shift. We were expected to wear clean and ironed shirt and pants, and during the check, we even lifted our pant legs to show our black non-slip shoes and matching socks. Our aprons had to be spotless and equipped with essentials: a lighter, a pen, a $20 bank, and a wine key. Failure to comply with these standards meant facing a write-up or even being sent home. This military-style routine applied to both a.m. and p.m. shifts, underscoring the high standards set by the establishment.

Even though it functioned as a brewery restaurant, it upheld remarkably high standards, reflecting the owner's vast experience from opening dozens of unique restaurants in the 80s. Additionally, the General Manager, K2, a graduate of Johnson and Wales, brought her own rigor to the establishment, having previously worked at various venues known for their extremely high standards. Unlike the college bar, where the bartenders were the stars of the show, here it was the management team.

Taz, the bar manager, towered at 6'4". A seasoned deep-sea diver and long-time bar professional, he was known for his humor and no-nonsense attitude. Then there was Rhonda, the former General Manager who had stepped down to the role of Assistant General Manager. She was all business, displaying little emotion and observing the room with a hawk-like vigilance. Reading her was a challenge; she was intimidating, always dressed impeccably in a business skirt and jacket, and conducted pre-shift checks with meticulous attention to detail. Next in command was K2, the main boss. She was a whirlwind of energy, navigating the three levels of City Steam, including the comedy club in the basement and the top-floor kitchen, with ease—even in high heels. A small frame with a large presence, she was undaunted by confronting patrons twice her size and escorting them out without a moment's hesitation.

And then there was Art, the chef. His attire was a heavy contrast to the others: a bandana, cut-off jean shorts, and, notably, all-natural. Known for his crankiness and quick wit, Art worked alongside his team on the line, sweating through the busy shifts. Coming from a family deeply rooted in the restaurant business, Art's background would prove to be fortuitous for me later on. But at that moment, these were the formidable leaders I had to acquaint myself with. All had a history from which I would have the great opportunity to gain benefit.

Initially, I wasn't a standout server, but with each shift at City Steam, I improved steadily. I was "new meat," like in a Vietnam War movie. I was in the training program with another guy, Steve, and we were the new guys no one really cared to meet yet. Juggling my schedule proved challenging, especially on days when I had to arrive in Hartford hours early or after enduring a 7-hour stint in the dish pit at Nullis. At City Steam, being a newcomer meant fewer shifts due to the staff ranking system, so my hours were limited.

Determined to make a change, I saw an opportunity to leverage my new serving experience at City Steam to shift my role at Nullis. I approached Matt, the owner, and informed him about my serving job in Hartford, inquiring about any serving opportunities at Nullis. To my relief, he offered me a single Saturday shift. This meant my week now consisted of three serving shifts at City Steam, one at Nullis, and three days back in the dish pit. The uncertainty of how this hectic schedule would pan out loomed over me, but the allure of the serving income kept me motivated. Earning anywhere from \$100 to \$200 a night was new to me. I was rich every once in a while.

Working nights in Hartford also introduced me back to the vibrant after-work scene. My colleagues and I would often wind down at Lord Jim's, a speakeasy in the true sense of the word, it was a bar tucked away in an office building accessible via an escalator and a seemingly closed-off hallway. This extremely unassuming spot was a no-rules haven for hospitality workers and seasoned drinkers, many of whom had been turned away from more reputable establishments. Lord Jim's was more than just a bar; it was an escape, complete with a pool table and a jukebox that set the mood for our nightly retreats. However, this new routine also brought its own set of challenges. Mornings became a game of memory and assessment: Where had I ended up? Was my wallet still with me? How much of last night's earnings remained in my pocket, and who's that? These questions became as routine as the unpredictable nights that preceded them.

As I got better at serving, I began climbing the ranks, earning enough shifts to let go of two out of my three dishwashing commitments. No longer just the 'FNG' – "Fucking New Guy" – I was becoming an integral part of the team. My regular gig was every Thursday in City Steam's Comedy Club, a shift as unpredictable as comedy itself. Some nights, we'd have a crowd of 30; other times, barely five. As the lower-ranked server, I accepted these inconsistent evenings as a rite of passage.

Ely, the bartender during these comedy nights, had a history with the company stretching back to his teenage years as a busser and barback. Now around 46, he balanced bartending with a day job at an insurance company and a family at home. Despite his love for the bar scene, he wasn't a fan of the Thursday shifts in the comedy club. Sensing an opportunity when he half-joked about handing over the bartending role to me, I jumped at the chance. "See if Taz will train me, and I'll take over," I proposed eagerly, envisioning this as my breakthrough.

A week passed without any developments. When I nudged Ely about it, his surprise at my seriousness quickly turned into action. "I'll ask," he promised. Another week went by, and the verdict was not in my favor. Rumor had it that management wasn't too fond of me – perhaps my confidence had bordered on cockiness. It definitely did.

Determined to turn things around, I knew I needed to win over Taz, Rhonda, and K2. I became a model employee in their presence – running food, bussing tables, helping out wherever possible, and toning down my bravado. I also kept urging Ely to advocate for me. Our persistence paid off. Finally, they agreed: I was to train as a bartender in the comedy club. It was a small but significant victory in my journey at City Steam.

The next day, as my shift in the dish pit at Nullis was winding down around 3 p.m., I noticed the owner, Matt, engaged in a visibly stressful phone conversation. After hanging up, he huddled with some of the senior staff, looking more strained than usual. Curious, I asked a server about the commotion. "Andy quit," she informed me. Andy was the full-time bartender, and, as luck would have it, the part-time bartender was unavailable to cover the shift.

Seizing the moment, I approached Matt directly. "I can bartend," I told him confidently, adding, "I bartend over at City Steam." While this wasn't a complete fabrication—I had been promised training and a future position at City Steam—I hadn't yet had the chance to pour a single drink or stand behind the bar. Matt, however, didn't ask about these details.

Relief washed over his face as he realized he had an employee, me, who could potentially step into the role, even if just for the evening. He didn't question my experience; his concern was filling the gap urgently, and I had presented a timely solution. Lesson learned was opportunity comes from chaos if you act.

That night, Matt lent me one of his button-down shirts and I stepped behind the bar, feeling out of my depth. He quickly ran through the basics, pointing out the ice wells and bartending tools, and handing me a *Mr. Boston's Bartender's Guide* – a lifeline, considering my limited knowledge extended only to Jägerbombs and Jameson shots. The bartending tools might as well have been foreign objects to me, but I nodded along with fake confidence.

Fortunately, the bar was quiet that evening, with my tasks limited to pouring beers and wines for the servers. No cocktail orders yet, I thought, relieved. Then, two older gentlemen entered and settled at the bar. Greeting them with a mix of nervousness and feigned competence, I took their orders. One requested a Peroni – easy enough – but the other asked for a Rusty Nail. A what? His choice seemed almost like a deliberate test of my inexperienced skills.

These guys looked like they had been drinking at bars for 50 years and I knew they could see right through my facade.

"No problem," I replied with that fake confidence, quickly ducking down to consult the bartender's guide. "Drambuie and Scotch," I read. Feeling somewhat reassured, I mixed the drink and served it.

The man took a sip and immediately winced. "This isn't very good. Are you sure you know how to make these?" he questioned.

"Of course," I responded, trying to maintain my composure. He just shook his head. Thankfully, they were my last customers for the night.

As I stood there, book in hand, it dawned on me: I really needed to study this guide. I was officially a bartender now, albeit in the title more than skill. Far from being turned around, I was determined not to let my lack of experience hold me back. I never had before.

CHAPTER EIGHT

RAISING THE BAR

Ok, I was ready. I was a bartender now. Except in reality, I wasn't even close. The next time I had a serving shift on a Thursday in the comedy club, I cornered Ely.

"I'm bartending at Nullis now; let's kick start that training!" I suggested, hoping to accelerate my progress.

"Alright, I'll talk to Taz," he promised, referring to the bar manager.

Shortly after, Taz informed me that Mark had put in a good word for me to take over the Thursday night comedy bar shift.

"Ready to start training next week?" Taz asked.

I enthusiastically agreed, keen to dive in.

Now solely bartending at Nullis and having left serving and dishwashing behind, I began to grasp the basics of bartending, akin to familiarizing oneself with a new car. How to adjust the mirrors, where are the lights and wipers, etc. This experience at Nullis provided a gentle introduction to bartending essentials. However, when training in the comedy club commenced, I quickly realized my overconfidence. The club's menu featured 15 specialty drinks, catering to a crowd that enjoyed their liquor during shows. Relying on a cheat sheet for the initial shifts, I gradually found my footing, albeit in a less busy environment than anticipated.

Taz, sensing my potential and thinking forward, decided to extend my training to the main bar upstairs as a precautionary measure. This led to a few training sessions during lunch shifts. Meanwhile, my efforts to improve my standing had paid off – I was now the fourth-ranked server out of twenty, according to the weekly staff rankings determined in the managerial meetings.

Life in Hartford was becoming increasingly rewarding, but the logistics of commuting to the city and balancing my schedule grew more complex. Stan, one of the newer managers, and I quickly became good friends. Facing a recent breakup and in need of a new living situation, Stan proposed that we become roommates. We found an apartment in West Hartford with another friend of his, significantly simplifying my commute to City Steam. However, this new arrangement made traveling to Manchester for shifts at Nullis nearly impossible. Consequently, I decided to leave Nullis, move to West Hartford, and concentrate on advancing my bartending career in Hartford.

The main bar at City Steam resembled an old Cadillac: large, somewhat cumbersome, but spacious and with some rust. It was unlike any bar I had previously encountered, boasting over 20 seats and extending more than 60 feet in length. Stepping behind it for the first time, I felt a mix of excitement and timidness. Rob, the bartender tasked with my initial training, appeared somewhat disengaged yet remained cordial. He guided me through the opening routine: laying out mats, preparing an abundance of fruit, stocking juices and syrups, gathering a small mountain of ice, and other essential tasks. He had it timed pretty well, but right as we were finishing up, the doors opened and here came the lunch rush. The first drink I made on my first day was a frozen strawberry daiquiri and at that moment, I had hoped I would never have to make another.

Throughout the shift, Rob briefed me on the bar team dynamics. I was already familiar with Ely, but he introduced me to the part-timers: Matty, the IT specialist who never missed an opportunity to complain; Jay, the frat boy turned realtor; and Pete, a computer engineer who bartended at the service bar once a week, primarily to mingle with the female staff. Then there were the full-timers: Lee, an older gentleman whose unique quirks suggested he might be on the spectrum. He avoided alcohol, preferring a variety of flavored sodas, and adorned himself with more beads than one might find on Mr. T's neck. The team was rounded out by Katy and Missy, the bar's "mean girls" or, in another context, the boss ladies akin to prison rules. They thrived under pressure, dictating the pace and timing of when the volume bartenders should step aside, ensuring they maximized their earnings. Their efficiency at the bar was unmatched; Missy, in particular, wouldn't hesitate to bypass customers who weren't immediately ready to order or who fumbled their requests.

I soon learned the reason behind Rob's "I don't give a shit" attitude: he had recently submitted his resignation, which explained why Taz had me in training. This change presented an opportunity for me to secure a full-time position at the bar, moving away from serving on the floor. I recognized that while serving had its merits, I aspired for more within the hospitality industry, and bartending represented a significant step up.

I was now at City Steam full-time. One of the managers was my friend and roommate. I was high up on the totem pole on the server rankings and learning to bartend at all the bars. Rob was the Friday night comedy club bartender. I was offered a crack at it. It was one show, usually sold out at

200 plus and I had worked it as a server many times. I was ready to take on the challenge. The day came. I had a barback to pour beer. My job was cocktails and wine. I set up, the lights went down and guests came in all at once.

The tickets started coming. City Steam Rum Punch, French martini, Cosmo, and ten more drinks after that. That machine didn't stop. My guests started to arrive. I had five seats at the bar top. They wanted to order food and drinks while the machine was going off with servers staring at me, waiting for the drinks for their tables. This was insanity. Surely, no one expected me to give good service and knock out all these drinks for the entire club all at the same time.

I fought hard. Johnny Black rocks. Cosmo, sub Ketel One. Gray Goose soda splash cran, Margarita with salt, six lemon drop shots. Servers lined up, impatient for their drinks, while my bar patrons signaled for their next order. Behind me, comedians emerged from the green room, requesting sodas and dinner, all amidst the non-stop pace of the drink printer. "You want it? You've got it, sister." This was the essence of bartending—managing the chaos with skill and grace. Indeed, this whirlwind of activity, executed professionally, could very well define the craft.

"Holy shit, that just happened," I thought.

Taz came downstairs to count my drawers. "How was it?" he asked.

"Wow," I exclaimed, overwhelmed by the intensity of the shift.

"Yeah, it wasn't sold out tonight. Normally, it's busier. Don't worry, it will get busy," he reassured me.

I don't think he grasped the depth of my "wow," and I knew deep down I wasn't ready. I had to improve, to dominate this shift just as I had conquered my first sauté position at Black Eyed Sally's. Advancing in this business means rising to meet each new challenge head-on. The hospitality industry doesn't adapt to you; you must elevate yourself to its demands.

It was on me to enhance my skills to learn how to master this new challenge. Life or death? Maybe not in the literal sense, but in terms of career and livelihood, absolutely. Civilians might not see it that way, but this was the path I had chosen. My income, my sustenance, my ability to pay rent—all hinged on my performance. It's akin to professional sports: perform or get the hell out of the way. Your background, beliefs, race, gender, or sexual orientation don't matter. What matters is, can you do the job?

Absolutely, I can, or at least, I will be able to. I may not be as polished as I'd like, but I'm ready to get gritty, to be sharp-witted, to draw on whatever it takes to meet any challenge that comes my way. The bar was now my arena. Fueled by determination and a touch of anger, I was set on succeeding. I have been through some nasty shit. My fear was fading fast and I felt good about fast-tracking. The issue to come was exactly this. I had healing to do to be a better person in general, but it wasn't that part of my life yet. Let's fucking go.

Next up, facing the Mean Girls.

I had graduated to Saturday nights at the main bar, the prime slot, where the action was non-stop. The bar was always three patrons deep, buzzing with energy from either the live band or the DJ, interspersed with the occasional brawls and drunken antics. To stay on, I had to match the pace of Katy and

Missy or risk being sidelined. So, I hustled—mixing, shaking, rinsing, and, in moments of pure folly, leaping over the bar to break up fights.

Despite my efforts to keep pace, to me, it never seemed enough for the formidable duo. After a few weeks, feeling somewhat confident in my ability to manage the onslaught of Jägerbombs, Alabama Slammers, tequila, and Black Cadillacs, I was certain I was excelling. Then, Taz summoned me to his office one evening.

"How do you think you're doing?" he inquired.

"I'm doing great," I confidently boasted.

"You're not. If you don't improve, I'll have to take you off the bar," he stated bluntly. Reality check presented a crossroads: either continue in my delusion of competence and look for another job or confront my shortcomings and strive to improve.

I chose growth. I might not have been the sharpest tool in the shed, but I was aware of my ignorance. I was ready to learn, to "paint the fence" and "wax on, wax off." I was prepared to humble myself and absorb every lesson, every critique, determined to not just meet but exceed the expectations. The journey from ignorance to proficiency was about to begin, and I was all in.

I knew to combat the twins, I had to be a stronger bartender. I needed to be fast, proficient, creative and good with recipes and mixing but I also knew where I could beat them: hospitality. I knew I could gain some love by just being a friendly bartender like Ely, just faster and more proficient. I knew my drinks and I also started to get to know the guests. During my slow lunch shifts, I would experiment with flavors and drink specials. I would try all types of flavor combinations. I was going to be good at this.

I was also getting in with regulars.

One of the regulars who left an indelible mark on me was Brian, an African American man in his early fifties, though one could mistake him for being in his sixties or seventies. He claimed seat 101 as his own, where he ordered Dewar's on the rocks — always insisting it be filled to the brim. Brian was a fixture, arriving daily at the same time, a testament to his very steadfast routine.

He entertained us with stories, tipping with candies instead of cash, consuming around four to five drinks and six cigarettes while waiting for his bus. Brian was as consistent with his work as he was with his visits to the bar. However, his routine was disrupted the day he learned of the new state law requiring smokers to step outside. His displeasure was evident as he declared, "Mark my words, you won't see me in here again."

Given Brian's love for one free drink, generous pours, and our captive audience to his tales, I suspected his absence wouldn't last long. Sure enough, a few weeks later, Brian resumed his place at seat 101. As a non-smoker, the nightly ritual of my clothes and body smelling strongly of cigarettes and cigars had been unpleasant. Kind of crazy, considering at the time, almost everyone in the industry was a chain smoker. It was a way to get a quick break and have something to do during shift drinks. Moreover, the bar once attracted guests who primarily came to smoke. Implementing the smoking ban nearly tripled my earnings. Couples began to linger at the bar, enjoying full meals—a rarity before the law changed. Regrettably, I learned a few years after leaving City Steam that Brian had passed away, not even reaching 60.

I began to improve behind the bar, venturing into crafting drink specials during my lunch shifts. This experimentation was crucial in getting better at cocktail combinations, a process that involved a fair share of trial and error. Drawing inspiration from my kitchen experience, I played with flavors, gradually learning what worked and, more importantly, what didn't. My training had covered only the basics, and my tool kit was modest at City Steam, but these limitations did not deter me. I was on the path to improvement, relying on my innate hospitality skills to bridge any gaps in my bartending knowledge. Selling cologne to strangers had honed my ability to engage customers, making it a walk in the park to entice hungry and thirsty patrons with food and drink.

Night shifts presented a stark contrast. The bar would often be packed, with patrons standing three to four deep, all eager for service amidst the booming sounds from the DJ or live band. Nighttime bartending was about efficiency and speed, maintaining constant motion without colliding with other bartenders. The air was filled with shouts for shots, pointing at guests to take their turn and the anxious gazes of customers hoping to catch our attention next.

My efficiency at night had increased, and I had mastered the rhythm of bartending. This improvement led to more lucrative solo shifts, and before I knew it, I had transitioned to a full-time bartender. However, as I settled into this role, I found myself at a crossroads, uncertain of my next move. Bartending was enjoyable, and the fun of the job and even more intense, the fun after the job, had become my primary focus. Yet, a part of me yearned for something more, something to channel my restless energy. I toyed with the idea of revisiting screenwriting or even venturing into opening my own bar despite feeling unprepared for either path. These thoughts were my attempt to silence the internal tumult as my spirit yearned for freedom and adventure.

I recognized a duality within myself: my core being, serene and grounded, contrasted sharply with my ego, which was erratic and insatiable. These two aspects of my identity seemed to converse with me independently, each pulling in its direction. In attempts to calm my restless ego, especially to find some semblance of sleep, I often resorted to drinking heavily or embarking on escapades that demanded my full, undivided attention but were often too big to immerse me entirely. These were my methods of quieting the noise, of temporarily satisfying the part of me that craved constant stimulation and adventure.

CHAPTER NINE

PEARLS IN THE OYSTER

Entering into a relationship with the General Manager, K2 was reflective of the common workplace relationships within the restaurant world at the time. Our decision to move in together compounded the complexity of our dynamic. Admittedly, I was not the easiest person to live or work with, especially as I grew more confident in my abilities. K2, with her exceptional resilience and profound expertise in the restaurant industry, not only made our relationship enriching but also served as an invaluable mentor and confidante. Her discipline and knowledge were unparalleled.

However, blending our personal and professional lives eventually led to tensions that spilled over into our workplace. Minor disputes that started quietly at work would often follow us home, becoming a more regular occurrence. It was during this tumultuous period that an unexpected opportunity arose. The chef, having heard from his sister-in-law about a bartending opening at Max Downtown, suggested I consider it. "You're a solid hospitality professional and would likely excel there. Interested?" he inquired.

"Sure, I'll give it a shot," I replied. Max Downtown wasn't just any restaurant; it was the jewel of Hartford and perhaps even the state at the time, spearheaded by Richie Rosenthal. Under Rosenthal's guidance, what began as a single establishment in 1986 evolved into the Max Restaurant Group, a distinguished collection of eateries spanning Connecticut, Massachusetts, and Florida.

The Max Restaurant Group boasts an impressive portfolio of ten unique, successful establishments and an award-winning catering service. With a workforce of 900 and growing, the group's influence stretches from Max A Mia Ristorante in Avon, Connecticut to The Cooper Craft Kitchen & Bar in Palm Beach Gardens, Florida, showcasing its diverse and quality-driven dining experiences.

In need of a fresh start, this opportunity seemed like the perfect pivot.

I attended the interview, where I met Jason, the front-of-house manager, and managing partner Steve. Both were impeccably dressed, reflecting the venue's sophistication—an establishment that seemed plucked from a high-budget film I could barely afford to watch. The aura of luxury was noticeable right from the entrance. Steve made a brief appearance to greet me before leaving the interview in Jason's hands. Jason outlined the position they were offering, a full-time bartender role, along with his expectations. I stretched the truth about my experience, aware that a certain amount of embellishment is part and parcel of the interview process in our industry—a skill that often proves useful. Jason specified the dress code, requiring a white button-up shirt and a tie, mentioning he would provide the vest. Although I wasn't thrilled about the vest, I recognized it as part of embracing new challenges. He suggested, "Why don't you shadow a shift to see if it's a good fit for you?"

"Sounds good," I replied, eager to explore this opportunity.

I arrived the following day and was introduced to Valerie, a slender, blonde bartender in her early thirties. Her demeanor was notably refined, almost to the point of seeming rigid to me. As we began setting up the bar, she shared her backstory: she was aspiring to become a real estate agent and had previously managed at one of Max's sister restaurants. Valerie struck me as distinct from anyone I'd encountered in the industry thus far; her ambition seemed focused on networking with the affluent clientele, perhaps in hopes of finding a wealthy partner. This mindset was something I discovered was not entirely rare in this setting, but personally, I couldn't connect with her approach. Her perspective on hospitality seemed skewed towards personal gain rather than genuine service. The patrons, while predictably affluent, carried an air of arrogance that matched my expectations. Despite the staff's evident skills, I felt misplaced, recognizing both my unreadiness and lack of desire to adapt to this environment. Post-shift, when Jason inquired about my experience, I candidly shared that this job wasn't the right fit for me, returning the vest with gratitude. He asked me to wait a moment, then returned with Steve behind him. Steve, having heard about my reservations, suggested an alternative: The Max restaurant in West Hartford. Described as more relaxed and with a lively bar atmosphere, it seemed like a potentially better match. "Would you be interested in trying it out there?" he proposed.

"Sure," I responded, already set on exploring new opportunities.

I next met with Bob, the managing partner of the West Hartford restaurant, who, despite his sharp attire, had a more whimsical demeanor. Our conversation flowed easily, and soon, he introduced me to Bones, the bar manager and brother to Chef Art at City Steam. With Bones, hospitality ran in the family—Chef Art's wife bartended at this location, and Art's sister-in-law was a legendary bartender at Max Downtown. It was a genuine hospitality dynasty. Bones and I had a straightforward chat, after which he outlined my potential schedule, making it clear: no vest, no tie required—just the ability to keep up. I was drawn to the laid-back dress code and the vibe, so I thought, "Why not give it a shot?"

With that decision made, I notified City Steam of my departure and braced myself for a new chapter here, located in the heart of West Hartford. This area was the epitome of hustle and bustle, home to the affluent and the place to be seen. Lawyers, television personalities, and the local elite frequented the vibrant dining scene here, making it an exciting but also high-pressure prospect.

The team at this bar was exceptionally talented. Looking back, I affectionately think of the Max Restaurant Group as "Max U." Throughout his 35 years in the industry, Rich Rosenthal has been a pivotal figure in the Greater Hartford area, not just as a job creator but also as a mentor to many now-renowned chefs. These protégés include Billy Grant of Bricco; Dorjan of Treva and Avert, and Scott from Zohara, both of whom later formed the Doro group; and Dan, a former Trumbull Kitchen staffer who now owns the Oyster Club in Mystic and has served as President of the Connecticut Restaurant Association. Remarkably, I had the chance to work alongside three of these culinary giants at this Max location.

One day, I had the opportunity to meet Rich Rosenthal himself. He approached the bar, extended a warm welcome, and joked, "Hey Justin, nice to meet you. Welcome to the team. Shave that thing, just kidding," referring to the soul patch beneath my lower lip. My trainer immediately whispered, "He's not kidding," underlining Rich's blend of humor and high standards.

The bar team here, however, were the real stars. With a mix of personalities as diverse as their talent, the team included Nadine, who would later become a prominent figure at Connecticut Distributors, a branch of Breakthru Beverage; Chuck, a cranky and clever old-school barman with a slight limp who could insult you and you would hear it as a compliment; Mr. Smith, a hospitality legend known for drawing a crowd; and Bones, who dominated the service bar reminiscent of his brother, Chef Art when he was working the line. Despite the bar's compact size, the bartending team was large, and the earnings were substantial, often doubling or even tripling what I made in previous jobs, even after splitting tips among four to six bartenders. This bar catered to a clientele of affluent professionals who expected and received whatever they desired.

Even our barbacks and support staff were on track for elite careers. Andres and Atilio, two friends hailing from the same town in El Salvador, demonstrated versatility and dedication by working in all aspects of this restaurant, from the dish pit to running food and barbacking. Atilio, in time, advanced to become a bar manager at one of my venues and many more, currently operating a vibrant, speakeasy-esque cocktail bar. Andres has not only taken ownership of that bar but has also expanded his ventures to include several other unique concepts. Their journey from immigrants to business owners is truly remarkable. Similarly, a barback named Miguel started as a barback and carved out an impressive career for himself. He now serves as the general manager of one of Connecticut's premier restaurants.

The bar was bustling, bringing in guests who would go to great lengths for our attention and a taste of our fun cocktails. One incident I'll always remember happened when a woman was walking toward the exit, which was about 20 feet from the bar's main serving area. Suddenly, her knees gave way, and she collapsed, only to be swiftly caught by another patron. This quick-thinking guest shouted to us, "Quick, we need water and call an ambulance!" capturing everyone's attention. But then, without missing a beat, they added, "And I'll take a Cosmo and a Razztini!"

I couldn't help but think, "These people are insane."

During my time there, I had the opportunity to become well-versed in oysters, learning varieties from both the East and West coasts. East Coast selections included Blue Points, Wellfleet, Chincoteague, Malpeques, Island Creeks, Beau Soleils, and Cape May Salts. From the West Coast, we offered Kumamotos from Washington, Kusshis from British Columbia, Baynes Sounds, Fanny Bays, and Drakes Bays. Typically, East Coast oysters are known for their salty, briny flavor, presenting a paisley shape, narrow body, and a somewhat chewy texture. In contrast, West Coast oysters are characterized by their sweet taste, deep cups, plump bodies, and round shapes. Enjoying these oysters was more than just eating; it was an experience, one that our guests turned into an event.

Drinks were crafted with fresh juice—a novelty for me at the time. We used a press right behind the bar for on-the-spot freshness, elevating our cocktails to another level with Espresso Martinis, Razztinis, Cosmos, Watermelon Martinis, and Lemon Drops, all adorned with creative garnishes. Being the new bartender, I was tasked with restocking wines and bottled beers, a process that involved climbing up and downstairs to the wine storage and familiarizing myself quickly with various varietals and brands. The nights were long, often not ending until 4 a.m., without even factoring in after-work activities. This job introduced me to a whole new world, and I was thoroughly enjoying the ride. Despite working fewer hours, I was earning more money.

Life at home with K2 was generally great, yet sometimes, the monotony of lawn work and the lack of a clear goal weighed heavily on me. My drinking escalated rapidly. One night, I met a former coworker downtown for drinks, and before we knew it, we were catching a taxi to a bar a few towns over. Wisely, I had left my car behind. Calls and texts began pouring in, signaling it was time to return home, but I ignored them. I was too caught up in the fun. I told my buddy, "Just one more, then I'll head back." The next thing I knew, I was being carried into an emergency room, jolted awake as the EMT accidentally rammed my broken leg into the doorframe. Laid out on the table, I overheard the doctor informing K2, "This is going to hurt, but I don't think he needs anything." She concurred. My leg was forcefully realigned, and I was informed surgery was imminent. The following day, I awoke in a hospital gown, bedridden and surrounded by medical staff, being wheeled to my room where my Aunt Linda and K2 awaited. Though dreading what was to come, I knew I needed to hear it, given my total blackout.

The story of how I ended up there was secondhand. I wasn't present mentally, but the story was crazy to me. After somehow returning to my car in Hartford, which I don't recall, I struggled unsuccessfully to unlock my door. Fortunately, Denny, a City Steam bartender I worked with, spotted me in my hammered state. Despite being a nuisance, he insisted on driving me home. In his Scion, which resembled a boxy minivan, I became unbearably obnoxious. Impatient, I chose to exit the moving vehicle. Denny, hearing the door and feeling a bump, stopped to find I had vanished. My attempt to jump out resulted in a twisted ankle, subsequently run over by the car. Both my tibia and fibula were broken, albeit without breaking the skin, and my ankle rotated 360 degrees, displacing the surrounding tendons.

Surgery involved realigning my bones with a steel plate, repositioning my foot, and securing the tendons with screws, which were later removed, though the plate remained. I was benched for six months, unsure how I would walk or if I'd ever run again, let alone tend bar. This realization struck me hard. What was truly wrong with me? By some miracle, I hadn't taken to the road, sparing myself and potentially others from greater harm. The incident left me with ample time for reflection. Jobless since the Max's Bar needed a working bartender, and with K2's understandable frustration tempered by her supportive presence, I was spared additional guilt. My pressing concern wasn't the excessive drinking but the lack of direction. I recognized a dire need for purpose, something to command my focus, something greater than myself. Yet, before I could pursue such a purpose, I had to confront whether I could recover from this ordeal.

CHAPTER TEN

THE CHINESE PROVERB

Being sidelined from work, burdened with medical debt, directionless, and left with nothing but my own thoughts, I found myself in a very low place. However, as often happens in my life, I stumbled upon a metaphor that served as a lifeline in my sea of despair. It was a Chinese proverb that I clung to as if I were hanging from a cliff a thousand feet high, with a thousand venomous snakes below, waiting for my fall to drag me to hell. The proverb goes like this:

A farmer and his son had a beloved stallion that was essential for their livelihood. One day, the horse escaped, prompting their neighbors to lament, "Your horse has escaped; what unfortunate luck!" The farmer simply responded, "Perhaps, perhaps not. Time will tell."

Shortly thereafter, the horse returned, bringing several wild mares with him. This time, the neighbors exclaimed in joy, "Your horse has returned and brought additional horses with him. What fantastic luck!" Yet again, the farmer remarked, "Perhaps, perhaps not. Time will tell."

In the following days, while attempting to tame one of the mares, the farmer's son was thrown off and broke his leg. The neighbors, once more, expressed their sympathy, "Your son has broken his leg; what terrible luck!"

The farmer maintained his perspective, "Perhaps, perhaps not. Time will tell."

A few weeks later, as soldiers from the national army passed through the village, recruiting all able-bodied young men, the farmer's son was exempt due to his injury. The neighbors proclaimed, "Your son has been spared from conscription; what incredible luck!" To this, the farmer replied, "Perhaps, perhaps not. Time will tell."

This proverb became a beacon of wisdom for me, a guideline, and a reminder that the nature of fortune is ever-changing and unpredictable. It taught me to view my circumstances with a broader perspective, acknowledging that today's misfortune might be tomorrow's blessing.

Here is how.

At 31, I found myself at a crossroads, thinking my days of adventure were behind me. My depression deepened due to the lack of physical activity, and my days were spent at my aunt and uncle's house, largely consumed by smoking pot and watching UConn Basketball clinch a national championship. It was clear something had to change. As I gradually gained the ability to stand on my injured leg, albeit with a boot, a glimmer of hope emerged when my former bartending venue expressed a need for a service bartender. This role, confined to a makeshift bar no larger than seven feet by seven feet, with just an ice well and tap system, was perfectly suited to my limited mobility. It allowed me to sit, mix a few drinks, pour some beers, engage in brief chats, and earn a bit of money—signaling a return to some form of normalcy.

During this period, I dedicated a lot of time to reading in the service bar— a challenging task for me in general, but one I now had ample time for. I immersed myself in magazines covering a range of interests, from drinks and filmmaking to restaurants and philosophy, keeping my mind active and engaged.

As my condition improved and I was able to discard the boot, my mobility increased significantly. I defied predictions that I might never run again, motivated by a stubborn refusal to be limited by others' expectations. Before long, I was running three to five miles every other day, regaining my physical strength and setting the stage for my return to work.

Compiling a resume, I set out in search of employment. However, finding a bartending position proved challenging, as these roles are often held tightly, vacated only by those who retire or, in rare cases, jump out of moving cars. As expected, the Max restaurant had filled my position, leaving me to explore new opportunities.

Then, I caught wind of a new venture in a lifestyle center—a modern twist on the outdoor mall—in South Windsor, a town that straddled the line between affluence and middle-class living. A New American contemporary restaurant was in the works, hiring for all positions as it was still under construction. It was an opportunity I couldn't pass up.

I attended the open hiring session, stepping into an empty storefront transformed temporarily into a recruitment hall. A small group of people, diverse in age, race, and gender, gathered around a folding table, taking papers as prospective staff. Approaching the table, I was promptly asked, "What position are you applying for?"

"Bartending," I replied confidently.

They handed me an application, along with a personality test and a competency exam, mentioning that completing everything should take around 45 minutes. It felt like taking my GED test all over again.

I settled into a chair, furiously working through the tests and filling out the application before submitting them along with my resume. Another man, dressed head-to-toe in professional attire very much like Dockers' advertisements, reviewed my paperwork.

"And what position are you applying for?" he inquired.

"Bartending," I repeated.

He glanced over my forms and responded, somewhat dismissively, "We're actually fully staffed for bartenders, but thank you."

I was pissed and visibly frustrated, thinking, "That would have been useful to know an hour ago." I nodded, trying to disguise my irritation, and turned to leave.

Then, from behind me, a call stopped me in my tracks. "Hey," he shouted. "You've worked for the Max group?"

"Yes," I confirmed, turning back towards him.

"Alright, we can bring you on board," he decided almost instantly. "Training starts in two weeks, but we're in the middle of building the bar. If you're interested, you could help with that and start earlier."

I agreed without hesitation. "No problem," I said, my eagerness to dive back into work clear in my voice.

I arrived at the construction site where the future restaurant was rapidly taking shape. The floor was yet to be laid, and the new equipment still sported its protective wrapping. JP, introduced as the general manager, was the Dockers guy and was already there waiting for me. A former police officer, JP had managed another establishment nearby before taking the leadership role at Burtons Grill, my new place of employment. Though he wasn't one for many words, his intentions and expectations were always clear. JP would later become one of my favorite general managers and a model for leadership as I advanced in my own career. But at that moment, my task was hands-on and foundational: installing shelves in the bar cooler and arranging shelving on the back bar. It was clear there was a significant amount of groundwork to be completed before I could serve my first drink.

Having both setup and closed bars in the past, constructing one from the ground up was a new challenge for me. JP placed his trust in me to make key decisions regarding the bar's layout and flow. For the first time, my experience felt like the most valuable in the room, transforming this task into a significant opportunity. This was to be fortuitous.

The training sessions were rigorous and thorough, held daily alongside tests. We engaged in meetings and interactive games, outlining expectations and delving into the company's philosophy—a structured and comprehensive approach to onboarding.

Burtons Grill & Bar was the brainchild of some talented restaurateurs, one of whom is Kevin Harron, a seasoned professional with over 30 years in the restaurant industry. Harron's extensive background included roles at notable brands such as Legal Sea Foods, Kelly's Roast Beef, and Outback Steakhouse. As the head of Outback franchisee Tedesco-KPH Partnership, he expanded his portfolio to 17 restaurants, including one in development. These establishments were later acquired by the franchisor in 1999 for an estimated $71 million, marking the inception of Burtons.

After a stint on Outback's corporate team and at Kelly's, Harron felt a compelling urge to create his own concept. He collaborated with Kevin Rowell, my favorite all-time hospitality person, and Pat Gordon to establish Burtons Grill & Bar, drawing the attention of investors like Peter Lynch from Fidelity Investments. The founders recognized a gap in the market for baby boomers who had outgrown the offerings of casual dining chains. Inspired by Houston's, they envisioned Burtons as a destination for "active, discerning adults" seeking high-quality food and wine—a vision that Denise Baron Herrera, the Vice President of Food and Beverage at Burtons, works tirelessly to fulfill.

This establishment was more than just a job; it was a masterclass in the industry for me, offering both invaluable lessons and financial rewards. I was poised to excel at this bar, ready to harness my skills and truly make a mark. My experience at Max's had ingrained in me the essence of hospitality, while Burtons was about to teach me about building a strong foundation and fostering growth.

Having a top-notch chef like Denise Baron Herrera solidified the success of the group as well as mine. Chef Denise was and is a talented powerhouse.

I might have been knocked down, but I was far from defeated. This opportunity was set to open doors to realms I hadn't yet imagined. Having Max's restaurant listed on my resume might just have been the lifeline I needed. Perhaps this was my chance to dive back into the world I loved, to excel in bartending, to alleviate my depression, to rediscover my direction, and maybe, just maybe, to find happiness again.

"Perhaps, perhaps not. Time will tell."

CHAPTER ELEVEN

CRAFTING A CAREER

I was now a long way from home. Cutting onions at a small pizza place, frying tortilla chips in a chain kitchen, wearing a cheap tux and hoping for a Mafioso at a wedding to give me a tip for an extra piece of cake; I was a bartender now. I was given an arsenal of knowledge and I built this bar. I nested. I was confident because I knew my shit, I was charismatic and the food was awesome. I had no fear and that was not the best-case scenario.

We underwent rigorous training, and I mastered the menu inside and out. Equipped with a wealth of knowledge and exceptional food, my task was straightforward: sell the product and sell myself. Easy enough. On opening day, I manned the point side of the bar—the spot closest to the entrance, designed exclusively for serving guests as opposed to handling the service well or managing glassware in the middle. The service well was the engine room, but the point was the stage. I had enough experience slinging drinks and managing service bars to work efficiently, but this was my chance to truly stand out. And stand out, I did. It wasn't long before the bar was packed with guests eagerly waiting for seats in my corner. I did more than just entertain and fulfill orders; I orchestrated the flow of guests, signaling when and where seats were becoming available. My colleagues, Maureen

(Mo), who expertly managed the service bar most nights and later became a celebrated winemaker, and Allison, who provided steadfast support in the middle and was the queen of kind, were in perfect sync with me. Together, we turned that bar into a staple. It wasn't long before we saw the dining room start to fill up as well, a transition I'm confident we participated in.

This period marked my coming of age in the bar world. Initially, the thrill of the new venture left me feeling fulfilled. However, my confidence quickly morphed into arrogance. Instead of showing empathy towards those struggling to keep pace, I looked down on them. Watching others try to capitalize on the regulars I had worked hard to cultivate left a sour taste in my mouth, and I began to resent it. I excelled in hospitality but fell short as a team player to those outside the bar area, becoming the very type of person I had once contended with. This was not the person I wanted to be. At first, my home life improved—I was less stressed. But that too began to change as I found myself with time to spare, working only four shifts a week while earning a full-time income.

What's next? After work, I found myself increasingly eager to go out, a desire reminiscent of the behavior that once left me with a bum leg. Recognizing the danger signs, I decided to channel my energies into filmmaking once more. With the connections made at the bar, I landed gigs creating commercials for local TV, including a series for a New Balance store chain owned by a pair of hard-working guys I met at the bar. They were hard-working like me, and before I knew it, their commercials were airing locally.

Then there was the documentary project which was a different beast. (SIDE QUEST #3 BUSKING THE SYSTEM). A coworker at Burtons Grill, Chris, who would later co-found Hartford's first real cocktail bar, Little River Restoratives, struck me as the perfect partner as co-writer for this venture alongside a childhood friend, Mike. Together, we produced and directed *Busking the System*, a documentary exploring the lives of subway musicians in NYC. The film, born from my fascination with street performers during my time in the city, followed three musicians from across the country attempting to carve out a niche in the underground music scene of NYC. We sourced our subjects from Craigslist and spent nearly three months documenting their journey alongside interviews with established street artists. Although *Busking the System* found its way into some markets, I remained a bartender at Burtons, my creative drive undiminished.

The Silk City Flick Fest, a film festival I initiated in my hometown of Manchester, was another creative outlet. Attracting submissions from around the globe, it featured screenings across multiple venues, accompanied by parties and panels. Meanwhile, Burtons Grill began to expand. As part of this growth, I was selected to train the bar team at a new venue in Boston, a task that involved setting up the bar, training staff, and assisting with the opening. This assignment offered a deep dive into Boston's bar scene and allowed me to work with future industry leaders including Steve Arkilean of Johnny Kono's five-star dive bar, Danny Azzarello of Crack'd Coffee and Kitchen, and Nick Harron, kitchen and bar.

Following Boston, my focus returned to the film and festival circuit, along with opening additional Burtons locations, including one in Virginia Beach. This assignment proved different; the debauchery among the higher-level crew was surprising, and one day's excessive indulgence left me stealthily vomiting and napping in a minivan while trying to teach people how to be professional.

Despite these escapades, my professional life was thriving. I was influential in menu development, enjoyed generous tips and gifts from patrons, and saw potential in my film endeavors, traveling to L.A. for festivals and discussions about the documentary. I was learning again about regional cuisine. The tacos and sushi were on another level. The fusion was amazing but the pizza sucked.

However, Burtons began to feel stagnant, and when a contact from my film festival days, now managing a new Spotlight Theater in downtown Hartford's Front Street development, offered me the chance to combine my passions for restaurants and movies, I jumped at the opportunity. I was his only contact of my caliber who knew the industry and he needed someone to help this venture succeed. Another confirmation that relationships meant everything. This was one of the first theaters that was going to allow meals and cocktails inside the theater. Despite my experience, I was unprepared for the leadership role this new adventure demanded.

Front Street's revitalization had stalled due to the recession, lying dormant for four years. Yet, with its rich history and phased development plan incorporating dining, entertainment, residential living, and educational facilities, it promised a vibrant future. This development, named for a historic thoroughfare, had begun transforming Hartford's riverfront into a dynamic district, blending nostalgia with modern urban living. If it could catch on. Spotlight Theater was going to lead the way and I was going to lead it.

I played a pivotal role in shaping every facet of this new venture, from the menu and team building to the operational flow, decor, and overarching theme. My experiences had positioned me for such a role, yet in hindsight, I was akin to Luke Skywalker in *The Empire Strikes Back*—eager yet never finished my training and incomplete for the responsibilities I had assumed.

I enlisted a badass line cook as head chef, whose talent and toughness were undeniable. However, her readiness to lead and preference for enjoyment over management soon became apparent issues. My choice for assistant manager was a highly organized and intelligent host, yet her ambitions lay beyond the hospitality industry, leaving her less committed to our collective goals. The rest of the team were even more wild cards, each bringing their own unpredictability to the table. Our food and drinks were adventurous, reflecting our enthusiasm and creativity, but in the hands of our inexperienced team, these ambitions stretched us too thin, making our exciting vision a challenging reality to execute efficiently.

Around 2012, our movie theater bar and restaurant introduced some inventive dishes, one of my proudest being the loaded mashed potato waffle. We'd take mashed potatoes, cook them in a waffle iron, and then garnish with cheddar cheese, sour cream, and chives. It was one of the unique side dishes that set us apart at that time. Now, nothing special.

The bar was my pride and joy, built from the ground up under my sole direction. It was a canvas for my creativity, where each drink was meticulously crafted for perfect balance and distinct uniqueness, inspired by the cinematic world. The menu was a tribute to iconic films, featuring creations like the Trainspotting, a playful variation on the Penicillin cocktail, named after the Scottish indie film. I had the opportunity to experiment with a wide array of ingredients, including seasonally infused Pisco, lemongrass, and a variety of other fun unique flavors, spirits and concoctions.

The restaurant quickly became busier than anyone anticipated, outdrawing even the cinema itself. I was both excited by our success and dismayed by our inability to consistently manage it due to a lack of proper team dynamics, insufficient systems in place, and my own shortcomings in leadership.

My approach was more about setting high expectations without providing the necessary guidance and support, which wasn't ideal for a team primarily composed of individuals looking for work in a movie theater setting. However, the bar was thriving, gaining recognition for our cocktail creativity. We found ourselves contenders in "best of" cocktail competitions in local media, which began to build my reputation in the local bar scene. This success was a double-edged sword, highlighting both our achievements and the areas where we fell short.

I had also relocated my film festival to Hartford to align with my work at the theater and launched a comedy festival the following year. My schedule was packed, but this busyness meant I wasn't taking the time to learn and grow from my experiences. Instead, I became wrapped up in my own hype, unaware that I was on the brink of a much-needed reality check.

CHAPTER TWELVE

ANYONE KNOW A CHEF?

Credit: Winter Caplanson

We were thriving at Spotlight Theater, becoming a hot spot for happy hour
and dinner, with the theater itself gradually gaining traction. Our location
was strategic, situated across the street from the convention center, the
Marriott, and the science center, which funneled a steady stream of patrons
our way during events. Despite being a movie theater bar, we started to build

a respectable reputation, outperforming expectations. We were, metaphorically speaking, wearing pants too big for us but managing to keep them up, surprisingly for a ragtag group of rookies. The subsequent arrival of The Capital Grille across the street, a high-end steakhouse chain owned by Darden Restaurants, marked a new chapter for Front Street.

The management from The Capital Grille made it a point to visit us during their opening phase, extending courtesies at our bar before systematically recruiting our standout staff members. This experience introduced me to the harsh reality of poaching in the hospitality industry, adding yet another lesson to my growing repertoire. In my only glory, their second night open, they sent one of the former employees over to borrow toilet paper.

Around this time, my drinking started to gain momentum again. Not only was I consuming alcohol excessively, but I was also doing so at work and alongside my staff. One particularly sobering moment came after a night of such imbibing when I awoke with no memory of how I had gotten home or closed the restaurant. Facing the theater managers and the general manager the next day, my embarrassment was very apparent, similar only to the shame I felt after breaking my leg. It was a clear sign that it was time for me to move on. My readiness to lead without supervision was in question, not just on a professional level but personally as well. At that point, I convinced myself that what I needed was a new challenge and guidance, not fully acknowledging the deeper issues I had been avoiding. K2, supportive as ever and busy with her own career, hadn't noticed the extent of my struggles, which I had been hiding very deep within, accumulated over many years.

Fortuitously, in 2013, a friend and a former manager from my City Steam days named Anthony made a surprise visit to the bar where I was working. He began to share his plans about opening a new restaurant as a managing partner alongside Jay Dumond, one of the founding owners of City Steam and godfather to many in Hartford's hospitality scene. The concept was a diner-style bar and restaurant offering breakfast, lunch, and dinner, located in a neighborhood of the affluent town of West Hartford. He then offered me the position of his second-in-command, responsible for developing the bar program. At that moment, I recognized that it was the right time for me to move on. Looking back, I realize that my life potentially relied on the move.

The diner was set to be named Blue Plate Kitchen, paying homage to the quintessential American diner experience but with a gourmet twist, serving breakfast, lunch, and dinner. This venture represented his dream, and initially, it captivated me. I was eager to return to what I excel at, and I am passionate about bar development. With real experience now under my belt, I was ready to craft a bar that would align with and enhance the diner's unique vision—combining classic American breakfast and lunch offerings with a chef-driven dinner service.

I jumped into the history and art of classic cocktails, aiming to master them before introducing my own creative twists. This deep dive into cocktail tradition was not just about mixing drinks; it was about weaving the essence of Americana and the innovative spirit of the diner into every glass.

I took immense pride in the menu, showcasing twists on classics like a delicious Pomegranate Daiquiri, a refreshing Bermuda Swizzle. Falernum quickly became a cherished ingredient. An Old Fashioned with infused large ice cubes, a caper-infused local Vodka Martini garnished with sriracha, blue cheese, and bacon-stuffed olives. The boozy milkshakes--a Maple Whiskey Pancake shake, and a White Chocolate Pistachio shake were particularly fun to develop. Diving deep into the cocktail and bar scene, I felt truly inspired.

Assembling the team proved to be smoother than my experience with the movie theater bar. The selection of glassware, the wine list, and the layout of service all clicked into place effortlessly. Having built a bar from scratch four times before, I was well-versed in the initial steps. Yet, I was aware that more challenging times were ahead.

One morning, while I was at breakfast with Jay and Anthony, Jay received a phone call. After a brief absence, he returned to the table with a solemn expression, remaining silent. Anthony, concerned, broke the silence with a probing, "What's up?"

"We've just lost our chef," Jay announced, his tone grave.

This bombshell dropped a couple of months before our scheduled opening.

"So, what's our next move, anyone know a chef?" Anthony inquired, concern lacing his voice.

"I might have a solution," I proposed. Amid our breakfast meeting, I quickly sent a Facebook message to a chef we all knew. He had been a line cook at the Burtons in South Windsor, where I had worked, moved on to a sous chef position at City Steam, and then ascended to an executive chef role at a Burtons in Massachusetts. Rumor had it he had moved on, but his current residence was a mystery to me.

My message was straightforward: "Hey Chef, hope you're doing well. Where are you these days?"

He replied very swiftly, "Currently working at an inn in Rockport, Massachusetts."

My follow-up was direct, "Are you happy there?"

His response was promising, "I'm open to a conversation. What do you have?"

Securing Ben would be a significant victory. Not only is he knowledgeable and passionate about food, but he's also focused on personal and professional growth. His ambition and expertise would perfectly align with our concept.

I shared the promising news with Jay and Anthony, who were both receptive to the idea. Our need for a chef was urgent, and given our familiarity with Chef Ben and his proven culinary skills, he seemed like a viable candidate. Although we hadn't seen him in action since he transitioned from sous chef to executive chef, I was confident in the extensive training Burtons provided. Convinced of his potential, we transitioned from a Facebook chat to a phone conversation in a matter of minutes. The call went really well, and he expressed enthusiasm about joining our team. We initially spoke in November, and by December, he began commuting from Massachusetts to Connecticut on a weekly basis, eventually starting full-time in January to prepare for our upcoming launch.

The menu at Blue Plate Kitchen was both exciting and challenging. It featured a diverse range of dishes, including challah French toast, various regional omelets and Benedicts, pancakes, eggs cooked to order, and toasters at every table for breakfast. Lunch offered a variety of sandwiches and appetizers, while the dinner menu was expansive, highlighted by daily-changing blue plate specials written on a blackboard. Despite the freshness and quality of the food, managing such an extensive menu across three meal services in a kitchen with only a 14-foot cook line and a small walk-in was incredibly challenging.

We somehow managed to pull it off. Brunch became a colossal undertaking. On Sundays alone, I found myself juicing at least two cases of oranges to keep up with demand. We served 400-500 guests within a six-hour span. Anthony tirelessly navigated the restaurant, engaging with guests at every opportunity, while Chef Ben, who also serves as a pastor, let loose a stream of expletives and blasphemies from the expo station. Offering Bloody Mary flights seemed brilliant in theory but proved to be a logistical nightmare in practice.

A significant complication was the number of decision-makers. The dynamic of having three meal services introduced a variety of opinions and second-guessing. The husband-and-wife ownership team often had conflicting views, each bringing their expertise and perspective to the table. The managing partner and the chef also had their own distinct opinions. Discussions often revolved around minor details, such as when to remove toasters from tables or which channels to play on the TVs, even if to have them on at all, detracting from more critical operational concerns. This abundance of talent and input led to a cluttered decision-making process.

Despite the fun aspects of the job and the high quality of both the food and the drinks, the stress of managing these complexities outweighed the enjoyment. The chef's culinary creations were excellent, my cocktails were well-received, and the decor and Anthony's systems were commendable. However, we overcomplicated things, leading to a depletion of confidence in our restaurant's identity. I learned here that everything needs to be extremely and clearly defined and communicated to staff as well as guests. I grew to have tremendous respect for Chef Ben, Anthony, Jay, and Lisa as we faced these challenges together.

Blue Plate Kitchen reignited my passion for bartending, serving as a crucial turning point that brought me back to what I love most. Despite the challenges we faced, which stemmed more from timing and the clash of five passionate creative minds attempting to be overly pragmatic, it was a learning experience. It was like having a mix of excellent ingredients that, unfortunately, didn't come together to create a harmonious dish.

My cocktail menu began to draw attention, not just locally but also within the broader liquor industry. An unexpected opportunity came my way when Nadine, a former colleague now working for a major liquor distributor in the state, invited me to participate in an iron bartending competition. Up until that moment, the concept of a bartending competition, let alone an iron bar competition, was foreign to me. Intrigued, I accepted her offer.

Nadine explained that I could assemble a team, and she provided all the necessary details. I reached out to a former coworker and another bartender I had previously worked with, both relatively new to the scene, who were happy to let me lead. The competition centered around Malibu coconut rum and took place at a rooftop bar in the city's center, featuring a DJ, judges, and a festive atmosphere.

Surrounded by teams from various Hartford County bars, we stood at our station, equipped with bar tools and a bottle of Malibu. At the signal, a sheet covering a table laden with fresh fruits, juices, liqueurs, herbs, and unique ingredients was removed. I immediately spotted a large pineapple and a fresh piece of ginger among the offerings. After a frenzied rush to collect ingredients, we crafted our cocktail and submitted it for judgment within the ten-minute timeframe. We also received points for garnish and name, so I grabbed some edible flowers and named the drink "Ginger Leigh Better."

The competition culminated in a tie between our creation and a cocktail presented by a team of three young bartenders, scantily clad, reflecting their workplace uniform. The tiebreaker involved crafting a shot for the DJ to judge. Anticipating the DJ's potential bias, we focused on crafting an irresistibly delicious shot. Our strategy involved using a watermelon to create a luge for the shot. After a suspenseful pause, our creation was declared the winner.

This victory in my first-ever bartending competition was exhilarating, instantly fueling my competitive spirit and building my confidence on my professional path. It marked the beginning of my deep dive into the world of competitive bartending, a journey I embraced wholeheartedly.

As time passed, it became evident that despite my fondness for Blue Plate Kitchen, there was little room for growth or change. After a year and some reflection, I recognized it was time to pursue new horizons and explore the full potential of my bartending career.

CHAPTER THIRTEEN

BEHIND THE MUSIC

Blue Plate Kitchen brought me back to the bar. It was my driving passion. It was a blessing to be able to rekindle that fire. The other issues aside were more of a timing thing than anything else along with five passionate creative people trying overly to be pragmatic and to get it right. A recipe of ingredients that are all wonderful but just don't taste like a balanced dish.

I decided to put the word out: I was ready for a new challenge. With a solid skill set under my belt, I was confident in my abilities but unsure where I would fit best next. It wasn't until later that I realized I had developed a reputation in my field. I knew how to run things smoothly and build a restaurant. A former guest who had made a name for herself in the catering business for years had recently joined a new venture in downtown Hartford. She heard that I was looking for opportunities and, knowing my expertise in managing bars, she arranged an interview with the owners for me. During the interview, I made it clear: I had the knowledge and the drive to succeed. They mentioned they had already selected a restaurant manager but were in need of someone to oversee the bar setup. Initially disappointed by their decision, I still saw the potential for growth, my passion for bartending, and remembered my favorite Chinese proverb for perspective.

Accepting the position, I joined the team of a venue that was expanding with a second location. The original spot in Norfolk, CT was an acclaimed music and dining destination, attracting an eclectic mix of artists like Art Garfunkel, Robert Cray, Deer Tick, and Chris Robinson. From rising stars to past famous performers on solo ventures, it had it all. Infinity Music Halls' decision to establish a presence on Front Street in Hartford resonated with me, especially since I had been part of the first restaurant to open there three and a half years earlier. The offer was promising, with decent compensation, a committed team, and ample potential for success.

The moment I truly felt star struck occurred just once. The kitchen was situated on the second floor, and accessing the downstairs dining room and bar required descending a staircase that led backstage before veering sharply left into the restaurant. This route often allowed glimpses of bands preparing to perform. One evening, as I carried food down to the restaurant, I reached the bottom of the stairs and stopped in my tracks. The Bacon Brothers were scheduled to perform that night, and just as I arrived, they were gearing up to take the stage. My gaze met Kevin Bacon's eyes as I stepped off the last stair. For a brief three seconds, which seemed to stretch into an eternity, I was utterly captivated. Shaking off the trance, I continued with my duties, but that moment lingered—there I was, face to face with Kevin Bacon. I grew up with Kevin Bacon.

I designed these bars with a focus on elegance, uniqueness, concept, and efficiency. The wine selection was engaging, the beers were an ever-changing array of top-tier craft options, and the cocktails were a mix of delicious, well-balanced, and inventive creations. The main bar was dope in itself, while the hall bar and the service bar on the mezzanine effortlessly mirrored the main bar's capabilities. My goal was achieved.

This success didn't go unnoticed. I soon found myself on the radar of liquor suppliers and distributors, receiving invitations to competitions and events. I vividly recall my first contest representing Infinity Music Hall, where the challenge was to showcase a new product from Hartford Flavor Company, known for its flavored liquors. I was the newcomer among established members of the bar community, setting up between Johnny and Rich, both respected bar managers I had heard about, with Johnny being a stranger until that day. They had elaborate setups with exquisite copper tools, making my simpler arrangement stand out. Looking back, that competition gathered some of Connecticut's finest bartenders, including Rich, a frequent winner in local media polls where I often placed second, and Johnny, whose reputation preceded him. To my surprise, Johnny expressed familiarity with my bar program and admiration for my work.

As the competition unfolded, with guests and judges sampling our creations, I had modest expectations amidst such esteemed company. Yet, to my astonishment, my name was announced as the winner. I approached the stage with calmness and restraint, a demeanor I would maintain as my signature in accepting future accolades, consciously avoiding any showboating but acknowledging, "I deserve to be here." That victory was a mix of luck and hard work, acknowledging that while my competitors were just as deserving, that day was mine. This win was the start of many successes at competitions on behalf of Infinity Music Hall, marking a significant period of recognition and achievement in my career.

In the competitive circuit, my success was real. Among the many contests, the Faith Middleton Martini Schmooze stood out as a pinnacle event, drawing in some of the most recognized bar programs. Faith Middleton, a name I was initially unfamiliar with, hosted a renowned NPR food and drink show, making victory in this competition a prestigious accolade. The setup was intense: 600-700 attendees, each with a vote, meant we needed to prepare a vast quantity of drinks. Unlike our more prepared competitors who batched their cocktails for easy serving, we approached the challenge with a rookie's enthusiasm, opting to craft each drink individually.

Determined and with no fear, my team and I dove in headfirst. I engaged with every patron, ensuring each cocktail was mixed, shaken, and served with a personal touch. As the event progressed, the physical toll became apparent—my fingers ached from the cold, skin cracked around my fingers, my voice weakened, and my smile strained. Yet, I maintained a genuine connection with each of the 600-plus guests, opting for freshly shaken cocktails for everyone.

When Faith Middleton took the stage to announce the winner, anticipation filled the room. Her speech felt endless, but eventually, she revealed the winner: Justin Morales from Infinity Music Hall. My response was measured; I maintained composure, calmly accepted the award, thanked my team, and exited the stage. This victory solidified my reputation not just as a skilled bartender but as a legit competitor. Winning this competition fueled my competitive spirit, leaving me eager for the next challenge.

Following the Faith Middleton competition, I achieved victory in several notable contests. Pisco Porton presented an enticing challenge: sell a specified number of cases and earn a trip to their distillery and vineyard in Peru. Confident in my abilities, I thought, "No problem," and indeed, we met the target. The notion that I, a kid from the north end who grew up with nothing and less of a future, was now headed on an all-expenses-paid trip to Peru was astonishing and exciting.

I secured my passport and embarked on an adventure unlike any I had experienced before. I had traversed the country in a dilapidated VW, explored the U.K. and Northern Europe by hitchhiking, and camped out in a tent, but this journey was distinct. My familiarity with the language was nonexistent, and my understanding of the culture was superficial at best. Sure, I had heard of the Nazca Lines and Machu Picchu, but such landmarks hardly encapsulate an entire country's culture, right? Indeed, they do not. I was on the verge of falling in love with a people just as I had in Ireland, London, Mexico, and across the U.S. I was about to discover that this world is brimming with incredibly wonderful individuals, and that those who do not venture far from home might mistakenly believe there are only a few good souls amid a sea of less favorable ones.

Peru was nothing short of incredible. Our journey brought us along the Pacific beaches, then ventured deep into the country, revealing towering mountains and expansive deserts, including a surreal oasis. Having lived in Arizona, I thought I knew deserts, but the silence here was profound, a void where, if blind, one might believe existence itself was a myth.

The night before our desert adventure, we indulged in Passion Fruit Pisco Sours at our hotel, a beverage so deceptively smooth that it betrayed its potency. The following morning, faced with the almost impossible task of joining a bus tour to the oasis for a dune buggy ride across the sand dunes, I found myself in dire need of dispelling the previous night's excess. Despite my efforts, remnants lingered as we embarked, sipping on El Chilcanos—Pisco, ginger ale, lime juice, and Angostura bitters—my now-favorite drink.

The village was built around a small body of water, an oasis in the middle of the desert. Our group of seven clambered into a deceptively basic dune buggy, driven by a spirited old man who navigated the dunes with a fearlessness surpassing any rollercoaster's thrill, compounded by a distinct lack of safety assurances. You could tell the old driver loved it when our butts clenched. Battling the urge to vomit from the residual Pisco, I closed my eyes and hoped for the best. During a pause to admire the desert, I discreetly distanced myself to eliminate the last of the previous night's indulgence, half-joking that my DNA might remain there for millennia, a testament to this moment of perfect nothingness—the kind of profound emptiness I would never encounter again.

My Peruvian odyssey also introduced me to the local cuisine: guinea pig, cow heart, and delicious ceviche. My favorite was *causa,* a classic Peruvian dish that you will find in any Peruvian restaurant worldwide. With layers of mashed potatoes, avocados, and a dollop of tuna salad on top, this potato dish makes for a hearty meal on its own. Yet, beyond the culinary experiences, I found a deeper connection with Peru. I came to understand and appreciate its culture, developed a profound affinity for Pisco, and left with a part of Peru forever etched in my heart.

During my time at Infinity, an opportunity arose for a brewery tour in Belgium, thanks to a local beer distributor where my Aunt Linda worked. We journeyed through Belgium, savoring beers and visiting breweries, including a monastery renowned for its hop cultivation and exceptional brewing. The trip extended to Paris, where we explored cocktail bars and historic sites and escargot.

Upon my return to Connecticut, I was offered the position of restaurant manager at Infinity. The owners were seeking a change, and I felt prepared for the challenge. My experiences—both triumphs and setbacks—had equipped me with valuable lessons. We boasted a skilled culinary team, dedicated wait staff, and a strong bar team, together achieving noteworthy success and innovation.

Even as restaurant manager, I remained deeply involved with the bar, diving further into the world of mixology. One of our suppliers treated me to an unforgettable experience at Tales of the Cocktail in New Orleans, an annual gathering for cocktail and spirits industry professionals. The event solidified my commitment to my career path, featuring pool parties, encounters with cocktail legends like Beach Bum Berry, and memorable moments at the

Carousel Bar in the Hotel Monteleone. I had not only entered the bar culture, I had become a part of it.

Now I was ready to put myself out there in this world and create my own restaurant. I had worked in Hartford a long time. One of the things I realized Hartford did not have was its own pizza identity. The cocktail scene was starting to take hold thanks to a former coworker's bar, Little River Restoratives. Craft pizza and craft cocktails were the perfect combination in my opinion. Both are great price points and both are loved. I had my eye on an empty spot across the street from Infinity Music Hall but I knew the rent would be far too much for me. But I dreamed and dreamed. I invented cocktails and pizzas. And I was ready.

CHAPTER FOURTEEN

SPRING CLEANING

I genuinely enjoyed my time at Infinity Music Hall on Front Street. Each night offered a unique experience, heavily influenced by the performing artists. Audiences for Chris Robinson of the Black Crowes differed markedly from those attending a Tommy Emmanuel concert. The venue had two distinct dining areas: one aimed at delivering an exceptional dining experience with limited time before the show and a five-star experience, then a 100-plus-seat mezzanine designed for guests to savor their meal quietly while enjoying the performance. With close to 300-350 covers across both floors, alongside managing dining services for the green room and artists, the operation was both exciting and very challenging. We had a capable team; Chefs Don and Dave were exceptionally skilled, making it a pleasure to work alongside them. Chef Dave, in particular, would become a lifelong friend and eventually a business partner.

The owner, while incredibly passionate about music and having established a reputable music hall in Norfolk, lacked restaurant-specific experience, which, in my view, sometimes led to problematic decision-making and honestly usually does. Following Chef Don's departure amidst a series of less favorable decisions despite Chef Dave's and my recommendations, the dream of my own venture—a pizza and cocktail venue—started to become an ambition. I found myself frequently looking across the street at an ideal vacant space, imagining its potential.

Motivated and with some help, I crafted a comprehensive business plan and developed a menu concept. I decided on The Wicked Brick as the name. The quest for financial backing was crucial. Not far from my envisioned location, a prime corner block was already leased for a new venture. A popular BBQ joint, thriving on a street behind Front Street, was set to upgrade and move into this space. The eatery, owned by a professional competitive eater and local Kansas City pit master I'll refer to as Badger had quickly become a sensation starting from a modest venue. Given their meteoric rise without traditional restaurant backgrounds, I considered the possibility of them partnering in The Wicked Brick project. I arranged a meeting with Badger at his current establishment on Arch Street to share my concept. He expressed interest but needed to discuss the proposal with his wife.

Meanwhile, my growing discontent at my current job—a familiar road I wished to avoid—prompted me to resign and seek a new, albeit temporary, role. My search led me to a rooftop bar in an affluent neighboring town in need of strong leadership. After submitting my resume, I secured an interview.

The bar was owned by a father-son duo, primarily involved in real estate development. It seemed they viewed the restaurant as a hobby or a shared interest, similar to supporting the same sports team, rather than a serious business endeavor, at least the father. During the interview, I was upfront about my ambitions to establish my own venue, engaging them with my experience and vision. They asked pointed, business-focused questions, leaving me confident in their interest and likely an offer.

I signed on, and two weeks later, I was given a tour of my new digs. It was a cool spot on the top floor of a pseudo lifestyle center/business complex downtown. I heard a lot about the chef and the bartender. The chef whom I will call O, was apparently very talented and also very moody. "Sounds like a chef," I thought. But it was hard for him to be a team player and get his numbers in on time or menus in on time. He is extremely talented in the kitchen, however and won one of the cooking shows on the Food Network. The bartender, TJ, was the real star of this show and really the one I needed on my side to get anything done.

As I was getting my tour on my first night, I walked through the kitchen and the chef was walking through the expo. I was introduced and said, "Hey chef, nice to meet you," and headed down; he just walked right by me with a very obvious "go fuck yourself." I have met cranky chefs, angry chefs, and ego-driven chefs. I'm not sure which phase of his life/career I had caught him in, so I didn't rush to judgment. I grew up with a chip on my shoulder but I knew this place would go nowhere with him at the helm, regardless of how good his plates were.

TJ, I met next. He also didn't seem to have too much time for me at first but did make a point to be welcoming. The bar was huge. It was a rectangle with four ice wells and an island in the middle filled with 100 different types of vodkas. The drinks going out were all in Martinis or pint glasses. It was a mix between a dive bar and a beach bar with a club vibe. The walls were large glass doors that opened up to a rooftop deck on each side, making it an open-air bar. Older women with younger men and older men with younger women. Lots of hair products and jewelry. Very loud generic beats played in the background. Not my type of hangout but the bar and deck were packed.

As I watched TJ, I quickly realized he was the machine. He orchestrated everything like where guests sat, what they drank and even who they talked to.

The staff was running around mostly cocktailing in between people dancing, taking selfies, and making out. The owner had told me he wanted to sell more food and wanted to be more of a restaurant. That was going to be a tough task. This was a party-style hook-up place. Nobody gave a shit about the crab cakes. Maybe some truffle fries at midnight but that's about it. This almost brought me back to the old College Bar days but for rich people. The only time I really saw people eating well is when Chef O had friends come in; he would spend 30 minutes building a beautiful raw bar tower and personally walk it out to the table, ignoring all the tickets in the kitchen while there was no ticket for that $150 tower.

Usually at the end of the night, the bathrooms were destroyed, people had to be kicked out, and we had to walk around the entire place to make sure no one was passed out somewhere. The bar floor was riddled with straw wrappers, bev naps, bottle caps, and just garbage everywhere, even though each bartender had a garbage can next to them. The start of the next shift was almost always pulling up receipts from guests who asked why they had a $200 charge on their card after they had closed out. We had to dig through the receipts to find that they had bought a round of shots and we had a signed slip. They would hang up, embarrassed.

One evening, while making my rounds on the crowded deck, I stumbled upon a scene that was all too common for the venue's party atmosphere. A couple was on one of our couches, the woman with her breast exposed, tank top pulled down, deeply engrossed in making out with her companion. I intervened, politely requesting, "Hey miss, please cover up." They paused to look at me, confusion apparent on her face, before resuming their embrace. I repeated my request more firmly, eliciting laughter from the man. Realizing the situation required further action, I informed them they needed to leave. At that moment, another woman from a nearby group approached, pleading with me not to eject her cousin, who was visiting from out of town.

Curious, I inquired about the man's identity, to which she admitted that she had no idea. I bluntly informed her that she was a shitty cousin and instructed both to leave. This incident was just another chapter in the series of chaotic evenings that defined the rooftop's nightlife.

There was a lot of work to do here. I was used to opening up places, not putting them on course. The staff made so much money I knew they didn't even want to.

I was about a month in. I was getting used to the hours, the music, and the drunk rich people. TJ and I were working together well and the two managers I was really there to mentor were coming together. I brought in some of my people whom I trusted to care and help change the culture. The staff's attitude was getting better and very important to my neurotic nature, the bar floors were clean of garbage every night. The bartenders were actually hitting the garbage cans. Progress was made in a short amount of time.

I had another meeting with the Badger in the meantime and we met in his BBQ spot. As we sat there, he said to me, "What do you think about putting the pizza place here? The lease is great and I have it for another six years.

Maybe you would be able to help me open the Front Street location. We have never done full service."

"I can see it," I said, "We may have to do some cosmetics but I'm down." We shook hands and I felt that we clearly sealed the deal. We briefly talked about the timeline and I left very excited about what the Badger and I could accomplish.

I went back to the rooftop bar and gave the expected news to the owners. They graciously understood but then mentioned that they had an idea. He asked me to meet him the next day at one of his properties in town. The next day, I found myself in a high-end strip mall, standing in a vacant space ripe for development. The suggestion was clear: "What if this was The Wicked Brick?" As I surveyed the area, ideas flooded my mind, their readiness to invest in my vision both exciting and flattering. However, a crucial factor held me back: the saturation of pizza places and bars within a two-mile radius. Contrarily, Hartford offered a less competitive landscape, not to mention the impending arrival of the University of Connecticut's satellite campus and other event venues where a pizza concept would thrive. With a heavy heart, I declined their offer, steadfast in my belief that Hartford was the more suitable location for my venture.

CHAPTER FIFTEEN

GOING IN BLIND

The Badger finally agreed to a finalizing meeting so we could put some things to bed. I sent over the business plan as well as my idea for the partnership split, etc. He told me to meet him and his wife at one of their locations. I showed up and he introduced me to his wife. We sat down and he began to explain the idea for the space, to my surprise, for the first time. We had a handshake agreement already. Maybe I was too old school. Mrs. Badger then stated she was hoping to use that space as a dessert bar and had it all mapped out already.

"Ok, so what the fuck am I doing here?" I thought. They started having the discussion in front of me which made it uncomfortable as hell. It turned a little heated and then finally, she said, "Fine, I don't want to have anything to do with it. We want to make sure it doesn't take up our time. This will be all you."

"Yes, I will run it completely and just fill you in," I said.

Again a handshake deal. No real numbers were discussed. It was already too awkward. I had a small victory. So, I left with that.

The plan was, I was to help manage the current BBQ location, help move one street over into the 21,000 square-feet location, and then help open their full-service bar area. Then, we would remodel the current location and I would run it. It would be a lot of work for me as I would soon find out, but the reward would be fantastic. So I thought.

I fulfilled my notice at the rooftop bar and left on great terms. I showed up for my first day at the barbeque joint, already hearing from some coworkers who had taken leadership positions here that they would work you to death and expect more from the grave. That didn't scare me and the prize was worth it.

I showed up for training and it was a holy shit moment. My initial impressions confirmed their accounts: I entered into utter chaos, reminiscent of a scene from *Apocalypse Now*. The staff operated under a *Lord of the Flies* mentality, with management barely holding on. The business thrived on sheer volume, leaving no room for reflection or improvement—survival was the goal.

By my sixth day, the situation deteriorated further when the general manager vanished with a $2,500 deposit, only to resurface later to return the funds. Suddenly, I found myself promoted to GM, lacking both the knowledge of the business and the respect of the staff.

I wasn't scared; I had dealt with shit my entire life and I had gold at the end of this shit-colored rainbow.

At this stage in my career, I had developed a successful approach for launching or revitalizing venues. I enlisted the help of former coworkers and employees whom I trusted to excel in their roles. I was fortunate that they believed in my vision, with skilled bartenders and servers accepting positions as cashiers, understanding that their loyalty and patience would be rewarded. This period required tough decisions: firing some staff, disciplining others, winning over many, and demonstrating to all that I was a different kind of leader—one who could not only keep pace but also genuinely listen and understand. My mantra became "Fuck around and find out," as I leveraged everything at my disposal to stabilize the operation. We reached a point where I could bring in a general manager to mentor, preparing for our transition to a larger venue.

In my role, I was introduced to the world of BBQ, a skill set both necessary and fascinating. My tasks included prepping pork butts, trimming brisket, managing two massive smokers, and making burnt ends—a delicacy that nearly became my downfall. At this point in my life, I had stopped eating mammals for about eight years. I would obviously eat it when I had to try things on a menu change or for business purposes but that was about it. My bloodwork and cholesterol health really benefited from this change.

During a shift we would run out of burnt ends consistently. People would often wait an extra 20-40 minutes for a new batch. So, I had to see what these things were all about. I had the cutter slice me a small piece to try so I could know what the hell we were selling. The moment I did, it was as if I entered a new realm of flavor—juicy, crispy, savory, and rich. It was the most satisfying food I had eaten up to this point of my life. I still did not eat certain meats with my diet but I made an exception for burnt ends. I ate a small amount every day. Literally within a month, I had to do some new bloodwork. The doctor called me in and said, "What the hell have you been doing?" I ratted myself out as my cholesterol spiked noticeably. I reset myself and got off the ends. In moderation, as a treat, I'm sure they are fine. Going cold turkey was always a better way for me.

Meanwhile, I pursued our future partnership for the pizza place, facing frustrating communication delays with Badger, who often responded late and off-topic. The workload was intense, involving not just long hours but also significant off-duty calls and planning sessions, especially for the bar layout at the new Front Street location. I took charge of hiring, designing the operational flow, and crafting the menu, setting the stage for a highly profitable bar operation. As we neared the launch of our renovated space, despite my contributions and the imminent opening, I still lacked a formal contract.

Now it was time for us to redesign and get my spot open. We did a light remodel. An extra-large pizza oven was delivered and put in by crane. The bar was a gorgeous subway tile. The bar book was my best work. The chef

I brought with me from the Music Hall created a perfect dough recipe with a four-day proofing which led to the perfect light but crispy leopard-style pizza and we had some really fun and perfectly balanced pies. We were not too far from opening and I still had no contract. I kept pushing but heard nothing back.

I had done my part. I helped facilitate the move. I built a solid bar program. I had redesigned the old location into a hip bar and dining spot. I hired and trained a capable team. Brought in a chef and kitchen team. It was all done. But one night before, I had no contract. I was told it was still in the works even though we had months. My options were to abandon all the hard work I had done plus the dream of concept or just hope Mr. and Mrs. Badger would do the right thing.

We opened. The reviews were on point and people were loving everything. Food and drink. I kept harping about a contract and finally got in contact with their lawyer in an email. Since they had a lawyer, I had a lawyer look at it.

"If this is your concept, you would be nuts to sign this," he said.

I didn't sign. But I kept working my ass off. At the time, I was just too thrilled that my dream had come to fruition. We had big-time industry people coming to our spot. Great chefs and bartenders. Servers and other hospitality people of note were in all the time. My playlist was always on point. Hell, I even put Cool Ranch Doritos in the cheese shakers to top pizzas with. It was everything I wanted despite not really owning any of it. I designed the bar top, which was paginated copper with great drinking quotes etched in it. I picked everything from the bar stools to what's on the menu. So much of this place spilled from me.

The largest insult came when I read in the local paper an interview with the Badger. He let the reporter know that the pizza place came to him in a dream. I had other industry pros whom I had told about this concept a year prior text me and call me to ask if I was ok.

I was. I was able to resist the pettiness. Again, I was living my dream. So far, it was so good.

Compartmentalizing the situation, I kept trying to be as good as we could be. We kept adding really cool pies and apps. My creativity along with my experience, I feel like I was peaking. The bar program was also gaining notoriety. I had just won a trip to Tales of the Cocktail from Brockman's Gin and won or placed in a few other events. Tales of the Cocktail is one of the world's largest annual trade conferences, festivals, and gatherings of cocktail and spirits industry professionals in New Orleans, Louisiana. If you have a good bar program you get in free to all the best parties and events. There is a spirit-sponsored pool party each day at the rooftop pool at the Hotel Monteleone. Let's just say you would not go in the pool sober after the second day or if sober, definitely not sane. It was so much fun. All those bartenders in one place, learning during the day and being who we were when class was dismissed.

I also won my second Faith Middleton Martini Schmooze which boasted almost 1000 people. The hardware, the trips and the print kept coming. I was on a roll. Then came the Connecticut Restaurant Association Awards. It was like the Oscars of the hospitality world in Connecticut. I was nominated for best mixologist. It was between me and three other extremely talented bartenders. It was the kind of awards that had a ceremony and the winners were announced live. I honestly didn't think I had a real shot compared to the pros I was in competition with. I knew them all well and they were really damn good.

I didn't have my contract but I had my pride and I had my pseudo freedom. Ironically, with the fame of the pizza place, the wife decided that she wanted to be a big part of it. So much for "We don't want anything to do with it."

At the time, the Badger had been working with a very popular and talented local chef to open a foodie-driven, high-end BBQ concept in West Hartford. At the same time, he decided to open a taco place in a very large space, aka the old Hot Tomato's in which I almost worked years prior. He was getting in his own head and wanted to be too big too fast, in my humble opinion. Sure enough, both of those locations closed.

My spot was being roped into the fold of the group more and more and the venue became less mine more and more and no contract made it a slap in the face more and more every day. Mrs. Badger wanted a dessert bar here.

Mr. Badger didn't know what he wanted. I gave them a concept and I designed it. I brought them two chefs. I brought them stability and mentored the GM who was to run their 21,000 sq. foot venue and so much more. My reward, as usual, was my lesson.

CHAPTER SIXTEEN

CRYING IN THE WALK-IN

Despite creating and working at a venue born from my dreams and having an incredibly supportive partner at home, moments of solitude often brought me to a state of deep unhappiness. Battling with depression and occasional sadness—attributed to what I presumed were standard life traumas—I tried to mask these feelings with work, alcohol, and a facade of resilience. Now older, I sought to confront and understand these feelings, prompting my first therapy visit since childhood. I went in expecting a bunch of bullshit. Day one was let's get to know you. I gave my story. Rattled it off like no biggie. "Wow," was her response. "Did you hear yourself?" she asked.

She outlined clear signs of PTSD contributing to my depression and how my tendency to suppress emotions led to further complications. Recognizing the truth in her analysis, I knew everything she was saying and I guess it didn't seem like there was another way. I ended up going two more times. I realized very quickly the value of the visit was having someone to talk to candidly and them saying it's okay not to be okay with all of this. I always healed the real nasty stuff solo. I also prescribed myself booze and distractions. I wasn't the best doctor but I would become serviceable. I took it upon myself to take responsibility for all that ailed me. It was and is okay not to be okay. But it's not okay not to try to manage it.

I knew I had a lot of work to do or there would be a good possibility I would not be here. This was a reality I had known since a very young age. I remember the day my mother had enough and tried to take her life when I was 16. My cousin took his own life. My sister smashed into a tree trying to take her own life at 19. At 13, I stared at a bottle of pills for 45 minutes, reasoning with myself, why not take them all. It was around and it's a real thought many people have. The hospitality industry, with its manic pace, late hours, and constant pressure, often attracts those battling mental health and addiction issues. It's a profession that can feel like a refuge for those of us with turbulent minds, offering a semblance of normalcy amidst chaos. However, the lifestyle—marked by substance use to wind up or down, the financial unpredictability, and the inherent stress of service—can exacerbate underlying problems.

Having money in your pocket after every shift, spending it because you're having fun, then waking up broke with the bills still there and now you have to go to work and not only perform but hope the restaurant is busy. Crying in the walk-in is a real saying in our business. It is the only place where someone can truly escape the madness and scream without being heard by the guests.

I had a friend-slash-coworker die from his addiction at 28. Another young guy who was a great young kid in his early 20s and whom I took with me to every place I opened.

I received an online message from a young bartender who had just started at the pizza place I had conceived of. He came across an old bar book I made. He was extremely complimentary and was looking for some feedback for some ideas he wanted to start running with. We spoke some bar nerd stuff and it was a very cool conversation. A year and a half later, he passed at the age of 30.

I have had those talks with employees that came in no shape to work, presenting the outcomes that succumb many of us who don't get our shit together in this business. It actually worked a couple of times. Sadly, not every time, and I have seen the bad part too much. It's real and I hope that I can help where and when I can share my story.

K2 and I broke up at this time. Though painful, it was a pivotal moment, prompting me to take responsibility for my well-being and commit to healing and growth. The journey is ongoing, but acknowledging the need for change was a crucial first step towards a healthier self. It was not too late but I had a lot to do. From my research, restaurant workers often fall into the top nine careers with jobs with mental health disorders and often number two to emergency room nurses. It's a great business for us but we can make it a place for us to get healthy at the same time.

My situation at work wasn't helping. Things were going well, in a way. My experiences at the BBQ spot and observing Mr. and Mrs. Badger build their chef-driven and taco ventures taught me something crucial: they crafted narratives to shield themselves from any blame, selecting scapegoats and pushing their constructed stories. I noticed how some individuals, despite questionable trustworthiness, managed to thrive under their wing. It was time. I needed to kick the shit out of demons and put myself in a place where I could help my hospitality family. I was so about survival for so long that it was me building up myself. I didn't live like a leader. But I needed to be healthy so I could. I gave my notice at the place that I had created and decided to start over. They cut my notice short and it was on to the next chapter everyone.

Sometime later, and I am saying this in no way out of joy, but as a matter of fact, the chef-driven spot closed, the taco place closed, the pizza place eventually closed and one of the managers that was saying only things that made the Badgers happy ended up stealing thousands of dollars from the company and the couple ended up getting a divorce. The Badger himself later courageously disclosed his struggles with addiction and depression publicly. It appears they were each battling personal demons, attempting to shield themselves from disintegration. However, this pursuit of self-preservation unwittingly resulted in numerous unintended victims. Despite these challenges, their original BBQ concept continues to thrive. To this day, I sincerely hope for their continued success and healing. It should be noted that the Badger would go to areas hit by disaster and help feed the people of the area. An example of the line we walk. The juxtaposition of who we are.

Soon after, I had started my next adventure. One of the things that was very important to me was mental and spiritual health. While I was in between avenues, I called up an old friend and coworker, Chef Ben. Ben, at this time, was the chef at a venue that he helped create, Bistro on Main, a casual gourmet French restaurant aimed to help individuals facing employment barriers—such as homelessness, domestic abuse, disabilities, and involvement with the criminal justice system—by providing them with culinary training and work experience. The concept was intriguing, and the food was exceptionally delicious. Chef Ben's talent and social commitment continued to flourish. When they offered some bar shifts, I eagerly accepted. It was an opportunity to engage in something meaningful while returning to what I loved—working behind the bar. Also, I had my first frog legs, as well as my last.

While I was there, we both expressed our thoughts on trying to figure out how to give a voice to people in our industry to vent and share experiences. How can we grow together? That's when we came up with HEARD which was in response to the industry's mental health challenges and following several suicides among peers. HEARD stands for Hospitality workers Engaging in community, Assisting each other, Restoring well-being, and Developing peer support skills. The group was created to provide a safe space for industry workers to discuss mental health, depression, anxiety, and the pressures unique to their profession, often exacerbated by substance use as a form of self-medication.

It was a small gesture but it was something. We met monthly or when we could. Sadly, it no longer exists and I miss it. It's a hell of a life to live a life in hell. It breaks my heart to see it happening.

HEARD was better than crying in the walk-in.

CHAPTER SEVENTEEN

RESURRECTING A GHOST

The owners of the rooftop bar I had previously consulted for contacted me during my time at the pizza bar. They shared exciting news about their recent property purchase in a rural area a few exits away. Among their acquisitions was a historic tavern, which had been closed for a decade and which they were eager to reopen. However, they were only interested in pursuing this project if I would join them; otherwise, they planned to rent it out. Given our positive past interactions and considering a change of pace from the city's hustle might be beneficial, I was intrigued. But the timing wasn't right as I tried to make the pizza bar come to life.

After my life changed, I agreed to take a look and chat. I visited the site with them. The tavern was essentially a hollow shell, with perilously open floorboards that could lead to an unfortunate accident if one wasn't careful. Despite its dilapidated state, the tavern's heart—a four-sided, three-level fireplace with an integrated oven—cast a spell on me. Built in the 1750s as an inn, the fireplace served as the building's core, embodying a rich history and untapped potential. I found myself excited by the possibilities.

At this point in my career, I could see the entire place already built, even though there were neither walls nor a floor. I have done this a million times. This canvas was the cleanest of all; ironically, the bones and heart were the oldest. We were set on honoring both: bringing this place into 2018 while maintaining the founder's spirit.

We kept the ceiling open and did not close the second floor so you could see the old beams, high ceiling, and four-sided fireplace reaching the sky. The bar was big. We took the most oversized room and built the most extensive bar. It was beautiful—so much room for activities.

The challenge was the kitchen. Not the layout but the quest for used equipment. One of my challenges with my new partners was that they were businessmen first. Not restaurant people. They wanted the chef and me to find used equipment. Used lowboys, sandwich prep stations, ovens, fryers, etc. Chef Pat and I went to back alleys that I thought we would never leave for some of the equipment. We found things not meant to be seen and tried to refurbish and clean them. The annoying part was that rumor had it that the father and son team had many millions in the bank. In the restaurant business, cheap is always more expensive. But we did it. We found everything we needed, and it was all beneficial. All were replaced with new ones within the year.

Now that that was done. It was time to create a menu. The original tavern had many things but was closed for ten years. The town was half old and half young. Whom do we appease? We started out trying to cater to plain old good restaurant people. I had pushed for a fun tavern vibe, but the owners wanted something elevated. We put parchment cod, duck and risotto, and mushroom toast on the menu. I loved and would eat all these things, but that was me. We found out very quickly that it wasn't what the town wanted.

We pivoted and adjusted quickly. The bar, on the other hand, was beautiful. It was carefully designed and curated. It was my best yet.

The team at the tavern was a mix of locals and seasoned professionals, but the bar staff, hailing from outside this small town, struggled to integrate. I was looking for a dynamic duo to bring cohesion to the bar. Unexpectedly, a solution presented itself through a friend and industry veteran who visited one night, introducing me to a bartender he recommended.

On the day of the interview, I met with Sam. She told me she wasn't challenged enough at her current location and was looking for more. I asked for her availability, and she told me she was available for one or two days and if it worked out, she could give me more. I wasn't one to audition for staff. If they wanted to join, then say so, but to put your toes in the water to see if you liked it, just wasn't my jam. I couldn't count on that, and I couldn't invest time in someone who didn't want to invest time in us. I excused myself, gave the interview to my assistant manager, and let him decide.

He hired her.

Sam quickly proved her worth as a server and bartender, mastering our high-volume environment and displaying a sharp wit I valued in hospitality professionals. Her dedication led her to leave her other job, committing fully to our team. As Sam became a central figure at the bar, the atmosphere among the staff began to harmonize, allowing me to divert my attention to refining other elements of the tavern's experience.

We hit our stride that first year, turning a decent profit and significantly boosting sales in a town that had been quiet for too long. I was mentally on the mend, coming into my own as a leader, and as things were looking up, I began to think about expanding our team and my professional growth. I organized a bourbon tour to Louisville to celebrate our success and deepen our industry knowledge, inviting Sam and JD, our other dependable full-time bartender, and other industry peers to join us.

The tour was nothing short of incredible. Industry insiders often receive VIP treatment, and we were no exception. Our visit to Angel's Envy Distillery included a special meet-up with its founder, Wes Henderson, and we left with personalized bottles from Michter's Distillery and selected picks from Four Roses. It was yet another testament to the perks of working in this industry.

The trip was such a success that I craved another one. We decided on Jalisco, Mexico, the birthplace of tequila. We set up a trip to visit the distillery of a tequila brand we crushed with at the tavern. There were four of us. The bartender from the TD bar, my long-time server friend who brought Sam into the tavern, and Sam herself. This trip was memorable. We met Illiana Partida of the Partida royalty. The Partida family's dedication to tequila production is deeply rooted, with the extended family owning roughly 500 hectares of agave. This tradition began in the 1960s when Iliana Partida's grandfather planted agave after returning from earning money in the United States. The commitment to continuous planting, regardless of the agave price, underscores the family's dedication to the craft of tequila production.

We saw a traditional still from the 1600s. We went to an ancient village recently found to be almost 3000 years old. We ate mangoes off the trees and drank some damn good tequila.

Now, working together for some time and going on two fantastic industry trips, Sam and I began to forge a stronger connection around this time, and it turned out we lived just down the road from each other. We started getting a drink after work and talking about everything. I had zero interest in continuing the initial interview with her, and now I was relying on her and interviewing her every night after work, learning more and more about her.

It was time to dive into the world of wine. After exploring South America for pisco, Central America for tequila, Europe for beer and cocktails, and Kentucky for bourbon, Napa Valley was the next destination on our list, eager to immerse ourselves in the world of fine wine. We planned visits to several renowned and historically significant vineyards. This trip was shaping up to be our biggest yet; our previous industry trips had caught the attention of our peers, and many were keen to join. The larger the group, the stronger our presence. We organized bus transportation, secured a spacious Airbnb, and made reservations at exquisite restaurants. Flights were booked, and the anticipation for an epic journey was palpable.

Business was humming smoothly, although there were murmurs in the news about a virus impacting the West Coast. It didn't seem pressing at the time—I'd heard similar alarms before and saw no reason to overreact unless it directly affected us. In restaurants, illness, be it the flu or a common cold, tends to sweep through the staff without exception, typically lasting no more than a couple of weeks. Given it was December/January, smack in the middle of the usual flu and cold season, we proceeded as normal, focusing on our upcoming adventure while keeping an eye on staff health for coverage purposes, etc.

CHAPTER EIGHTEEN

A ZERO'S JOURNEY

As stories about the emerging virus began to dominate the news, cases were escalating rapidly, though initially, the impact seemed distant, mainly outside the U.S., with individual cases being tracked from abroad. Hospitals were admitting patients, but there were no reported fatalities within the U.S., only abroad.

I vividly recall hearing the news on February 29th—a leap year, notably, and as I reflect four years later while writing this chapter, that date marks a significant memory. The first death in the U.S. due to the COVID-19 virus was reported in Washington state. This news struck me profoundly the next day during a table visit at the tavern. A guest introduced me to her companion from out of town. As I extended my hand in greeting, she mentioned she was visiting from Seattle.

"What the fuck!" were the words that ran through my mind. I wanted to pull my hand away as fast as I could, but the hospitality in me couldn't. I smiled and said, "Welcome." When she finally let go, I ran to the nearest hand sink and scrubbed.

I started getting messages from industry friends who had planned to go on the Napa wine adventure that maybe we should cancel. I remember messaging them back that we should not overreact because this will most likely be a two-week situation and everything will go as planned.

One week later, my partners from the Tavern and I were game-planning on whether we should plan for the governor to shut down restaurants like in other states. Closing the restaurant was so far from an option for me, but it seemed like we had to gameplan. We met, built a plan, and three days later, Governor Ned Lamont, New York Governor Andrew Cuomo, and New Jersey Governor Phil Murphy announced a significant measure in response to the coronavirus outbreak: the shutdown of Connecticut's businesses and restaurants starting Monday night. This coordinated decision across the tri-state area mandated that all affected establishments close by 8 p.m. Monday, March 15th, with restaurants restricted to offering only takeout and delivery services.

Coinciding with the Ides of March, the day Caesar was betrayed by his closest allies, this ironic twist mirrored our feelings as we faced the mandate to shut down. Despite the darkness of our situation, nature gave us a day of beautiful warm weather, perfect for day drinking. We rallied at a favorite industry bar in a neighboring town, joined by colleagues from various restaurants. This gathering was a celebration of camaraderie amid the uncertainty. It was a poignant yet beautiful day, a stark reminder of the harsh reason for our gathering and a testament to the strong bonds within the hospitality community. The industry folks, known for thriving in adversity, showcased their resilience and spirit and drank spirits like the pros we are. That day, surrounded by my industry family, was unforgettable — a sad occasion turned into a cherished memory.

We decided to sit with the entire staff and fill out unemployment paperwork so they could start collecting while we figured out our next step. I was sure it would still just be another two weeks. I'm glad I did not have a gambling problem anymore because I was so far off. It was very fortunate that the rooftop owner pushed for this. He was very business savvy, and the staff benefits. Two weeks later, Congress passed a 2.2 trillion-dollar relief package that gave people an extra $600 on top of what they were getting from their unemployment. Many people who tried to get on unemployment later had a tough time. As you can imagine, the unemployed workers were overwhelmed and quickly. Luckily, our team was set, and so was I, for the most part.

I was home and had money coming in. But I had nothing to do. You couldn't hang out with people in public. Life was isolating. Nature, however, seemed to enjoy the absence of us. Pollution started to wane. The information coming out was that you were allowed to have a pod of people like family around all the time, which was okay. We did a couple of HEARD meetings on Zoom to check in with people. I had a pod. It was Sam, JD, Chef Ben, one of our servers and friends named Meg, and a long-time bartender and friend Khalid. That was our gang.

Sam and I then really connected, going on many hikes to the lake, beaches, etc. Lots of outside things. It started being nice reconnecting with nature. Liquor stores and pizza places were still getting crushed with business. Delivery was a booming business. I still needed mental stimulation and verbal sparring. We started a podcast to satisfy our need for mental engagement and connection. So once a week, we loaded up with perfect bottles of booze and pizza and talked to each other for a couple of hours.

The initial episodes were chaotic, but we soon found a rhythm, delving into meaningful discussions and sharing industry stories. Named *A Zero's Journey,*

Credits: Sam Dziecol

our podcast aimed to highlight the adventurous yet often undervalued careers in the hospitality industry. What began as a project for our sanity quickly resonated with others in the industry, turning into a weekly ritual of storytelling, laughter, and sometimes tears, attracting thousands of listeners.

"Hey, love the podcasts."

"I listen to your podcast as I run."

"Can't wait for the next episode."

Sometimes people just quoted funny things that may have occurred on specific episodes. Now, we were doing it for many people who needed a distraction and were also out of work or having difficulty living through this shit. We were on every platform. It was wild to see 3000 downloads at one point. For just us idiots, was I speaking for myself, talking? We had to up our game, and we got more serious. We would rent outrageous Airbnbs for cheap and do destination podcasts. It was great. JD, however, started getting worse into the drinking while the rest of us were beginning to level out. Conversations were had. But sadly, nothing was getting through. I started to think that maybe it was time to stop but it was hard. It was therapy for us and others.

The podcast continued to evolve, featuring interviews with notable figures like Wes Henderson and Iliana Partida, chefs, bartenders, and doing holiday specials and roasts.

After three months, the call came to consider reopening the tavern for takeout, with rumors of outdoor dining soon becoming an option. It was time to transition from unemployment and adapt to the new normal of restaurants operating under pandemic conditions. This marked the beginning of a challenging yet hopeful phase.

Initially, the core team willing to forego unemployment benefits for the uncertainty of restaurant work included Sam, myself, Chef Pat and our sous chef. Although sales were modest, they were sufficient to cover our wages. The green light for outdoor dining service brought new challenges and opportunities. We assembled a small team of two servers and a host—not ideal, but enough to begin welcoming guests. Patrons were required to wear masks while moving through the restaurant to our patio, where tables were spaced six feet apart. Here, they could sit with their party of no more than six people and remove their masks. The stakes were high, as any deviation from these strict guidelines risked shutdown. Due to the limited staff, signage and directional arrows became a new fixture, and our team donned masks for 12 hours a day.

Public opinion on the virus and the response to it varied widely. Some feared immediate death upon exposure, while others speculated about government conspiracies involving the virus's origins and the imposition of masks as a means of control. Those of us in the service industry, along with grocery store employees, healthcare workers, and delivery drivers, found ourselves caught between these extremes, navigating constantly changing regulations and catering to the demands of both sides. This precarious balance made our jobs increasingly difficult, heightening tensions when the path to normalcy seemed more distant than ever.

We still did the podcast when we had time, mostly to vent. As things were about to open up, things were getting much worse. We had the death part starting to get under control, but it was the life part that was going to be the most challenging.

CHAPTER NINETEEN

NAVIGATING THE REAL STORM

Wearing a mask for 12 hours a day in summer, running around the restaurant from the bar to the kitchen to the patio and back to the host stand and repeat, was tough. Working the line in a hot kitchen in the summer with a mask on was worse. Pull the mask down to feel the warm air, take a sip of water and get back at it. This wasn't fun, but it wasn't even the worst part.

Throughout the summer, we operated outdoors, fortunate to have a sizable patio, and curbside takeout began to pick up. Regulations now permitted the sale of to-go cocktails alongside food, provided they were in a sealed container of up to a liter. We offered cocktails, wine, beer, and cocktail kits. Before the pandemic, we had been aging a particular old-fashioned using a recipe I developed years ago, infusing bourbon with black mission figs for about ten days, then aging it in a barrel with angostura and orange bitters, and a local birch liquor. I named it the Colonel's Old Fashioned at the tavern, and it usually took about two and a half weeks to perfect. I overlooked the aging cocktail in the chaos before the shutdown, focusing on minimizing perishables. Upon reopening, I discovered the batch had aged for three months, resulting in an exquisite version of the drink. Seizing the opportunity to sell cocktails to-go, I decided to bottle this exceptional batch. Given the preparation and aging time, I priced it at $75 per liter, with an additional option of a jar of cherries for $10, totaling nearly $90. We sold one, and then someone called and said my friend got this bottle of Colonel's Old Fashioned and loved it. Can I get one? This kept happening. Word of mouth just launched us. I had to start a wait list as I couldn't keep up. I had to limit it to one per guest. It was going gangbusters and at $90 a clip.

Fall was fast approaching, and in late September and fall, I was hitting up the hardware store weekly, filling five to seven propane tanks to keep our patio heaters in action. It was a new chore as my job as an operator changed every time a rule changed. But I did what I had to do. Unemployment with a $600 bonus seemed so much more enticing. But I never looked back. It was a good thing, too. Those who rode out the bonus had a much harder time acclimating back into the real world and an even harder time finding hours when the bonus was cut off. The temperature kept dropping week by week. Just in the nick of time, in mid-November, the state opened up to indoor dining with limited hours and seating. Tables six feet apart. Mask on until you get to your seat. Servers and employees still have masks on at all times. No one could sit at a bar, and a hundred other rules.

Most are not at their best when humans are afraid, confused, and unsure. Empathy is typically reserved for stronger people when times are tough. Most people can do it when life isn't so hard. A lot of people were scared. The rules changed so often and were frequently misconstrued or enforced so inconsistently that no one knew what to expect when entering a restaurant.

The arguments that 17-19-year-old hosts had to have as a front-line defense were nothing short of disgusting. I had to constantly police the host stand just to defend them from the brave maskless who couldn't grasp that we did not implement the rule. We were not the enemy, but these morons needed one, and the kids at the host stand were their most accessible sparring partners. It was ugly and got uglier and uglier. It didn't matter to us in the industry whether it was right or wrong. It was the law; to stay open and keep our jobs, we had to abide by it or be shut down. More and more, it became less about hospitality and more about who was going to give us shit and who was going to be excellent. This is the first time in my career that I have ever gotten into heated arguments with guests. I'm a hospitality guy first and foremost and have always taken it seriously, but when you are a dick and even more so a dick to young staff just trying to do their jobs, we were allowed to fire you—the best thing to ever come from Covid. We can now fire guests and fire guests we did.

Little by little came the changes. More people were allowed in. Parties could be more extensive. You could sit at the bar, but only if plexiglass separated the bartender and the guests. Shit kept getting weirder and weirder. We are a bizarre group of people, so we made it work and often in very ingenious ways. Some places were crushing it. If you owned a pizza place, Chinese place, or liquor store, you could probably retire after COVID-19. The places that were too old school to see a way to adjust quickly closed down. Many places were casualties. This opened the door for many new places and restaurants that industry veterans opened.

The landscape was to change, mainly for the better. Many people wouldn't even come back to the industry. This was good and bad. It was complicated as an old timer because it was a new generation of workforce not used to the grungy filthy nastiness of our industry. Instead, they came in ready to relax, and a sense of urgency was stupid. "It's only a burger. What's the big deal? They have only been sitting there for about five minutes. I'm sure someone was going to greet them eventually. What's the big deal?" If I showed the slightest bit of anger or frustration, the anxiety was just too much for them. It introduced a new, bright-eyed, hopeful group to the beautiful, awful world of hospitality and servitude. More than not, I had learned that the business was changing. We could do this differently. We could healthily do this. We just needed to work with intention. It had to be an artform and craft again. But I felt like a war veteran. Every day was a battle. My mentals were worn thin.

The challenge shifted as restrictions eased, and we were allowed to increase our capacity. The public was eager to return to normalcy, but the workforce hadn't rebounded. Experienced staff were scarce, and newcomers lacked the necessary skills, placing the burden on our core team: Sam, myself, server Meg, Chef Pat, Chef Ali, and a few others we could count on. This period was arguably the most demanding phase of the pandemic. With supply chain disruptions, we frequently ran out of essentials, straining our operations further. The gap between guests' expectations of "normal" and the reality of our situation was vast. Despite the external pressures, our team bonded like never before, drawing strength from one another.

Sam and I grew closer during this intense time, entering an unspoken relationship. We spent nearly every moment together, both at work and outside of it. Then, one day, Sam discovered a lump near her breast and, upon my urging, sought medical attention. The call came amid another hectic night, understaffed and overwhelmed. She took the call amidst the chaos, pacing through the dining room.

I went over to her as she hung up.

"What's up?" I asked

"I have cancer," she said as a matter of fact and walked right past me like we were 86 wings.

I went over to her and tried to figure out what to say. Drinks were still coming in, and guests kept sitting.

"Why don't you go home? " I said, assuming she needed the time to think, and I would jump on the bar.

"I need to work," she said. And went back to service.

For as wiped out as I was, Sam was just as wiped out and also told she had cancer. She impressed me because she handled it the way I would have. She was a tough industry person. Maybe not the healthiest way to be, but it is our way. Health insurance is not standard in our industry, so she also had to navigate that forest. Sam found a way to get insurance to cover her radiation treatments. She only missed one day of work and even covered her shift. This may sound sick on some levels, but that's a true industry pro. That's how it's done. At least in my/our unhealthy brain. During this time, she had to deal with radiation and unreasonable guests who would give her shit about dumb things while she knew she had breast cancer and worked full time. As a human, she deserved better. The most significant news was she beat it. She kicked that cancer's ass. Not only was she able to take volume, follow a recipe flawlessly and make no mistakes, she beat fucking cancer. I have a type, and it's badass industry people.

CHAPTER TWENTY

SAVOR EVERY UP AND DOWN

Credit: Lisa Nichols

Oh, to have owned a liquor store or a pizza joint when the world went sideways—I might have skipped straight to retirement, only to dive headfirst into opening my dive bar, cash only. As the world slowly staggered back to some semblance of routine and the iron grip of regulations began to loosen, we found ourselves in the awkward position of coaxing, or more accurately, begging, industry folks to return to the jungle.

I understand the hesitation at the same time to come back to work. Hours sucked, no benefits, many toxic mental health traits, and some very shitty operators. It was a mixed bag of things we loved and hated, and when separated from it long enough, it was like being away from a love-hate relationship.

I was running on fumes, questioning if there was another trail to blaze. The thrill of the game had dulled; I was merely moving through the motions, surviving rather than thriving. We were far from out of the woods, with the supply chain playing its version of roulette and pricing as stable as a drunk on a unicycle. And through it all, the guests remained blissfully unaware. Stuck in the muck of mask wars, I felt like a referee in a game I no longer enjoyed. The bottom line is that after 29 years, I was just about done.

Then came a curveball from my aunt and uncle—talk of supporting me with a dream if I had one. I was floored. What dream do I have? What would inspire me to take money from them? They slaved for it; it was theirs to enjoy. They wanted to be part of something that I could build. The thought of opening my own spirits brand had always danced around in my head—a tiny bar where I could be myself, serving up good vibes and better drinks. But the day I sold three more bottles of my Colonel's Cut, the light bulb exploded. Screw the bar. I was going to launch my brand. Let the world sip on what I've been brewing.

I started looking for someone that could make this how I wanted it on a large scale and that was affordable. I went to a company in the southern part of the state, and they said they could help, but they were way too slow and not moving the way I move. After a long time of contact with someone who used to own a local distillery, they introduced me to a couple of guys who were about to launch their liquors and would also be willing to produce my product. They were a little crazier, but maybe that's what I was looking for. We went back and forth to get the recipe right but eventually nailed it. The price was right, only as far as I knew, because I was the FNG (fucking new guy) to this world. We sourced the best bourbon mash bill and were about to contract for a couple of thousand bottles. It was far more than the advance I was to get from Bruce and Linda. Luckily, on March 16th, the stock market plummeted. I purchased as much stock as I could afford. Most of the market had made a decent comeback; from there, I could secure the remainder of the financing.

Now, for the soul of the project—the name. "Flavored Whiskey"? Too pedestrian. "Old Fashioned"? Not quite right. This was neither fish nor fowl; it demanded a new category. Enter "Rock and Rye," the old-timer's elixir, lurking in the shadows of prohibition lore. But here's the twist—Rock and Bourbon. A first of its kind, a nod to our bourbon-soaked heritage. But it needed a name that danced off the tongue, that could be slung across bars with the ease of "Titos and Soda." Thus, Up n Down Rock and Bourbon was born versatile and suggestive, with a nod to the highs and lows we chase daily. So I trademarked the name, and after a small legal battle, which I had to be the one to craft, and although I am not a lawyer, I won.

I contacted a local distributor. I had many. I have been selling booze for a long time at this point. I mistakenly thought I had some respectful capital. But the one company I really wanted to work with brushed me off very quickly. I put the word out, and three other distributors quickly started the wooing process. I went with the company that put in the most effort and was also the largest out of the group.

Up n Down hit the ground running, riding on the back of years of industry togetherness. It was local and had a story. The best part was it was being reordered. We opened with a cocktail contest at one of our favorite venues, which opened during COVID-19 and was owned by one of my favorite hospitality people. We had almost 20 competitors—all highly talented and well-respected bartenders in CT. I was more than honored; it could not have been a more perfect introduction to the world.

We have three very strong cocktails in the Up n Down stable. The Nightrider takes the lead, a robust blend of Up n Down Rock and Bourbon, coffee liqueur, and a dash of sweetness—think simple syrup or, for an extra kick, Tuaca or Licor 43—topped with fresh espresso and crowned with a lemon twist. It's a drink that packs a punch without the predictable vodka base. The other is the Secretariat, a drink I have been making for years but more recently with Up n Down. Up n Down, ginger ale, lemon juice, and mint. When I used bourbon prior, I used to add angostura and honey water, but Up n Down has both. The third daring was the Old Fashioned. Easy. Up n Down stirred and poured over ice with an orange twist and a cherry and— *voila!* These drinks are fun and easy, like I had 20 years ago.

Sam, now a crucial part of the team, took the helm of branding and marketing with an eye for what the label desperately needed—a refresh. Recognizing talent where it thrives, I reached out to Joe Capobianco, the mastermind behind my tattoos and an artist with a knack for the fantastic and edgy, to sketch our logo. To bring it all together, we enlisted the help of a former colleague turned graphic designer who also moonlights as a bartender, ensuring our brand wasn't just imagined but meticulously crafted. Sam continues to steer our marketing efforts, proving one of my wisest decisions yet has been to trust in her expertise and keep out of her way.

Our lineup has expanded to three distinct varieties, and we're now a presence in five states, with plans to introduce ready-to-drink options shortly. Sam's influence has been instrumental in shaping the brand's direction, turning Up n Down into not just a product but a story—a narrative woven through every bottle we sell.

Credit: Lisa Nichols

CHAPTER TWENTY ONE

TIO AND THE NIGHTHAWK

Credit: Lisa Nichols

Back in the day, at some point during my days of opening restaurants, I gained the moniker amongst my Spanish-speaking co-workers of "Tio." Tio means Uncle. I earned this name just by being there. I was accountable. Following through was almost the most critical thing about being a leader. If I said I was on it, I made it a point to get shit done before my staff had to ask again. I became Tio. I knew this was also an age gesture, but I didn't mind because at least I made it to this age. I knew many who didn't and some who did in our business were not doing too hot. In any case, here I was. Tio.

The year when things started to open up, the CRA, Connecticut Restaurant Association, decided to resume its annual awards and re-brand them as the Crazies. This was a minute after the world started coming out of their houses, and the hospitality industry was still in tatters. I didn't love the idea, but I understood why they were trying it. I nominated Sam as Bartender of the Year. She had gone through so much. She crushed the bar and dealt with all the changes and rules. She got yelled at for the masks bullshit and never broke. At the same time, she was going through radiation for breast cancer. She was the Bartender of the Year regardless of what God said. I knew this to be true. I have been doing this long enough to know she was it.

She didn't even make the ballot. That's when I felt this award stuff was shit. How can you pick from four people in a category when so many of us were trying to survive? I quickly realized no one's story was even being considered. Everyone in this industry was a winner in my mind, and I would make it so. I defied the CRA, not the nominees or winners, just the idea, and decided to make my own list of winners and as many of them as possible.

As a note, the CRA did its best to help us during COVID-19. I honestly don't know how successfully we would have bounced back without them. They were beyond lifeguards; they were the lighthouse. I am forever thankful for them. On the awards, their hearts were in the right place, but in my opinion, they swung too soon and missed.

This was October, and I decided to tell one story about one industry person every day until the new year. It was 87 days. That's 87 tales of toil, tears, and triumph, or, as I like to see it, a portrait gallery of the industry's backbone. Each day, I'd slap up a photo or three on the digital walls of social media, sketching out their stories. It wasn't long before my inbox became a shrine to nominations, each plea a testament to someone's grit, grace, or sheer stubbornness to keep the plates spinning, all deserving of the #thetios #industryaward.

The real kick, the pure joy of this whole thing, came when messages started to pour in. Some from the trenches alongside me, sharing tales of their comrades-in-arms; others, from the other side of the bar, patrons with stories of those who've served them memorably. It felt right—more than that, it felt necessary. After the new year started and the #thetios had ended, I was asked to continue after the new year, but truth be told, I was tapped out, and I was done. I was also still living my own story. Had I had a few more hands on deck, maybe the stories would've kept coming. Sharing those tales wasn't just a task; it was a privilege, a sacred duty to those living one shift at a time.

Nicknames are pretty common in our industry. A moniker born not from the trenches of service but the couches of quarantine. With the world on pause, I dived deep into the rabbit hole of streaming, finding solace in the absurdity of the movie *Step Brothers*. It became a ritual, a daily communion with Will Ferrell and John C. Reilly. One day, I joked to my team, "From now on, you call me Nighthawk," echoing my favorite line. My assistant general manager (AGM) renamed me on the point-of-sale (POS) system in a stroke of genius or perhaps mischief. So now, every shift begins with a reminder of those days, a smirk on my face as I log in as Nighthawk.

Picture this: I am wrestling with the POS, on the brink of declaring mutiny against technology. I'm on the phone with customer service, already envisioning all the other shit that I need to get done instead. "Listen, I'm the admin, Justin Morales," I insist, confused by their inability to locate me in the system.

"We can't proceed without confirming your identity," comes the exasperated reply.

Absurdity, this is tech support. I log in, dance through their hoops, and usher them into my online profile via chat.

And then, the kicker, "We only have an admin by the name of Nighthawk."

Silence on my end. A beat. Then, typed with the gravitas of a noir film's final reveal, "Who is Nighthawk?"

Here it comes, my moment of cinematic glory, delivered with all the solemnity a customer service call can muster: "I am Nighthawk."

And just like that, my alter ego was immortalized, not with a cape or a mask, but with a support ticket and a screenshot that'll live in the annals of my legend. "I am Nighthawk," echoed in the digital void, a statement of fact, a badge of honor, and a story that keeps giving.

CHAPTER TWENTY TWO

THE CALL BACK

The Tavern was running. We were back to the new normal. We had just enough staff in the right places, but it was not the roster we had prepared. We were still open five nights, with brunch on Saturday and Sunday. My AGM moved to the sister restaurant on the rooftop, so I was the only manager. From opening to closing, every shift was mine. I was hanging in there for the team's sake, but truth be told, I felt like a ghost. The pandemic and its relentless aftermath—this so-called "reconstruction"—had drained me to my core.

Eventually, Sam, now the bar manager, showcased her knack and intellect by handling opening and closing duties, giving me a few precious hours of relief. Yet, a proper day off remained a fantasy, and the idea of Sam and I taking a break together was outright fiction. During this stretch, I mulled over a few job proposals, tempted by the prospect of better pay and a decent benefits package. But the truth was, I lacked the zest for risk that marked my younger years. Plus, the team was loyal, and there remained a faint hope that my passion for the job would be rekindled. Our original sous chef had jetted to Peru to be with his family, leaving a void we filled with a familiar face—Chef Mickey, a line veteran. Mickey informed us about his upcoming time off for his impending paternity leave. Desperate for his expertise, we welcomed him back, handshake sealing the deal.

During Mickey's absence, we were short-handed, leaving me as the default fill-in. It had been a while since I'd tackled serious line work, though I had dabbled at the pizza place and a few other spots. Initially, it was manageable, even enjoyable. I geared up, tucked my Sharpie into my hat, and dove in. Still, the restaurant's daily grind—invoices, payroll, you name it—remained on my plate. Sam pitched in when possible. Still, she oversaw a bustling bar program and managed over forty seats. My return to the line was triumphant for some big nights, but the pace quickly took its toll. At 46, my last stint of serious kitchen work was at 26. My back ached, my knees screamed, dehydration set in, and overall, I felt physically spent—soft, to put it mildly. Mentally, I was still a demon. Reflecting on those grueling days, my thoughts drifted to the veteran chefs I worked with at an Italian restaurant years ago, men in their late sixties who were battle vets of the line. While I respected them at the time, I realize now they deserve far more honor for their tireless dedication.

I held down the fort in the kitchen for a few weeks until Mickey returned. While there was something satisfying about being on the line and tackling the dish pit, I was relieved to return to my domain in the front of the house.

I had grown in ways I couldn't have imagined. At this stage of my life, I intimately understood my heart, mind, body, and soul. I had stepped on enough nails to learn to watch my step. Yet, as much as I found my rightful place, I recognized the limits of my capacity. Life's vastness taught me humility; we control only our actions, not the narrative. Embracing continuous learning became my creed, knowing that thinking you've learned all life's lessons is the beginning of your end. We're here to contribute to the tapestry of others' lives, passing along our failures and successes. It's about creating a legacy of wisdom for those who follow. I'm not sure where the quote came from, but our responsibility as older mother fuckers is planting a tree and never planning to be relieved by its shade. I'm good with that. Just when this hit me, Chef Ben was on my caller ID.

"Hey Justin, how are you holding up?" Ben's intent was clear, even over the phone.

"Surviving," I replied, almost reflexively. The weight of the word was legit.

"Are you content where you are?" Ben's question pierced a bit deeper than I expected.

"I am working at Forge City Works and thinking of reopening the old Firebox, which is with a new concept, making it a social enterprise for the charity."

"I am very much looking to take a step back. I'm open if you think there is a bar manager type of position," I confessed.

He was straightforward, "Really? I had you locked in for our GM."

And there it was, my line in the sand. "Can't do it, sorry." It was time to find solace behind the bar again, where I belonged. With every tool at my disposal to make a difference in this industry, my heart wasn't in the fight anymore. That was my takeaway from the pandemic – my passion was the casualty.

CHAPTER TWENTY THREE

BORN AGAIN

Credit: Michael Leungevity

I folded. At my core, I'm stitched from the same cloth as this industry—hospitality runs through my veins. Plus, I'm the kind of guy who likes—no, needs—to steer the ship. The thought of sitting on the sidelines while others call the shots? I was too old and made too much self-progress to put myself in a position of unhappiness. I was already a boss, so why would I leave? I had been offered jobs for much more money, but I passed. I was drained, so why would I dig deep to muster the will to open another place? I know the dedication and the energy it takes to create a restaurant from scratch. This venue would be no different. If anything, it's even more complex.

The commitment, the soul it demands, to breathe life into a new space—it's monumental. And here Ben was, painting his vision of another social venture, meaning I'd have to flip the script on three decades of experience. Introducing untested methods to seasoned pros, sculpting systems from thin air—it's a monster task. This would be a huge undertaking. Sure.

Yet, the tavern's comfort, familiarity, and straightforward challenges were promises of an easier life. Could I bounce back there? Maybe. But the pull was too strong; I accepted Ben's proposition. We talked, ironed out some details, went over expectations, and then I gave my 60-day notice. Money was thrown at me to stay, which felt like an insult. Was I worth more? I don't remember you telling me. I know it's no one's job but mine to value myself; it was just the timing. I passed and set in motion my departure.

Sam was the clear successor for my position. Her potential was undeniable; she'd even been approached for the GM role at my new venture but chose to hone her skills further. Her work ethic was unmatched, and the owner was well-versed in what she brought to the table and where she could improve. I did not doubt that with a couple of months under my guidance, she'd navigate the ship as adeptly as anyone could. This was a straightforward choice.

Yet, the owner seemed addicted to convoluted maneuvers and secretive schemes, a strategy that, in my book, invariably backfires. On the other hand, openness and valuing loyalty yield dividends beyond measure...

I was off to open the restaurant formerly known as Firebox. To truly grasp the essence of Firebox, one must dive into the story of the influential Cary Wheaton. As the executive director of Billings Forge Community Works in Hartford, Cary masterfully intertwined her extensive background in the restaurant industry with a solid commitment to social activism. Initiated in 2006 under the watch of the Melville Charitable Trust, her vision was to invigorate an underprivileged Hartford sector by integrating restaurants, gardens, markets, and vocational training to dismantle employment barriers for residents.

Firebox, a trailblazer in the farm-to-table movement, succumbed after a 13-year run, its closure a direct consequence of the COVID-19 pandemic and the resultant economic turmoil. Firebox sought not only to delight with its remarkable local fare but also to spur job creation and community engagement. Despite valiant efforts to pivot to curbside pickup and limited outdoor seating, the pandemic's constraints—coupled with diminished patronage from neighboring entities and the lack of city events that once lured customers—proved too formidable. In its wake, Firebox left a void. The subsequent death of Cary Wheaton shortly after that marked the end of an era. Many super-talented industry persons had come through those doors.

Enter Ben. Ben had the closest fit to that glass slipper. He's got a heart as big as his appetite for making a difference, a deep love for food, and probably too many books on his nightstand. I was looking forward to teaming up with him again, though he was at the helm this time. I used to be a cynical line cook with a dirty mouth and a very rough edge. Although I had become a more effective leader through hard-earned lessons, this venture promised to redefine everything again.

Ben was on a mission to detoxify the hospitality industry, a noble yet significant endeavor. While a part of me clung to the belief that a touch of that very toxicity was necessary armor against the industry's chaos, I knew Ben was right; I just had a taste for it. Like when I had my first scotch at 21. It wants to be as good as it was portrayed in the movie *Swingers*, but I ended up loving all the whiskeys. You need to learn to love it.

That was just the restaurant side. But for the charity side, he wanted to go bigger. The restaurant, which was now decided to be called Fire by Forge, would be the real-life training ground after trainees passed the labs and classes we would be offering. We had to intertwine training with real time service periods now. This was going to be very interesting, and the challenges were starting.

The initial task was immersing myself in understanding the charity's core mission and operations. Many team members, having been with the organization for years, included former chefs — each profoundly passionate, committed, and fiercely protective of what they've built. I approached this not with a mindset to judge or instigate changes prematurely but to learn genuinely. I quickly realized the immense complexity involved in transforming lives through charity, and it became clear this ship was about to get a lot bigger.

Assembling the restaurant presented my second major challenge. While I've embarked on this task numerous times, integrating it with the charity's mission was uncharted territory. It felt like the tallest mountain I've ever faced, with no guide or sherpa to lead the way. Fortunately, I have never really been too afraid of falling. This time, however, I wouldn't be failing alone. I needed to be my absolute best.

CHAPTER TWENTY FOUR

THE MISSION

Credit: Winter Caplanson

Forge City Works serves people in the Hartford community with barriers to employment by providing job training in the food and hospitality industry to help them achieve sustainable careers.

This is the mission. This mission is foundational; everything hinges on it. The restaurant I'm tasked with launching must honor the legacy of Firebox and exceed it in quality, service excellence, and culinary innovation. Our catering operations must accommodate diverse needs, manage large-scale events, and meet various budget requirements. Yet, our guiding principle remains our mission. I lead our team to achieve these goals while staying true to our purpose. This involves cultivating a skilled and enlightened team and adapting to learning as we progress. This all has to be done while I learn how to do it. Most humans would get a monumental amount of anxiety. Luckily, that part of me broke many years ago.

I am again inside my weird comfort zone. Safe places and safe spaces were always uncomfortable for me. This new role promises intellectual volatility and challenges that will push me to the outer limits of my professional capacity. I'm ready to commit fully to this mission, battling against imposter syndrome by trusting my hard-earned experience. I'll dig deep because this cause—and the people it serves—deserve nothing less. They deserve it as much as I did but never received it, or I was too naive to see it. I accept my mission. I embrace this mission, so let's get it.

The building that housed the campus and, even more so, the actual restaurant was terrific. A historic landmark in Hartford, it originally housed a significant manufacturing business. Established in 1869 by Charles Billings and Christopher Spencer—both experienced metalworkers from Colt's Armory—the company initially focused on developing advanced die-forging techniques, including the board-drop hammer. Spencer departed in 1874 to start Hartford Machine Screw Co., leaving Billings to specialize the firm in forged mechanic's hand tools. By 1920, after Billings and Spencer had moved to a new facility, Hartford Automotive Parts Co. occupied the building, which was succeeded years later by Hart and Hegeman. Established in 1890, this latter company innovated early household electrical hardware, such as enclosed light switches and relays, right at the end of Mark Twain's time in Hartford.

The venue boasts abundant brickwork and large wooden beams that add to its historic charm. Tall windows flood the space with natural light, creating a striking view when illuminated from outside at night. The bar features a grand cathedral ceiling with exposed wooden beams reminiscent of beautiful, aged bones. It's inspiring to work in such a historic venue, having appreciated the importance of preserving such places during my last gig at the tavern. I'm honored to continue this tradition and contribute to the venue's incredible legacy.

It was time to breathe new life into the venue. We assembled a diverse team, ranging from seasoned professionals, aka cynical vets who knew the language, to newcomers fresh to the industry, soft and in no way ready for what would come their way. Together, we tackled the kitchen, bar, and dining room setup, all while finalizing the server alley, exhaust hood, plumbing, and flooring. Handling the variety of permits required creativity and constant improvisation. Ben, the eternal optimist, had originally aimed for a January 1 opening, but given it was already April, I realistically expected late May.

The push was intense but energizing. We developed menus and established systems simultaneously in a whirlwind of organized chaos, which I always loved. We started by opening the café, offering breakfast and lunch. A few weeks later, we introduced dinner and bar service. Meanwhile, our training program, which started in 2007, was undergoing significant changes, and we had to figure out how to integrate our trainees into the restaurant's day-to-day life. We had to adapt our plans on the fly, figure out the logistics of integrating training with live service, and create a living laboratory for learning as well as a destination restaurant. Every restaurant is its interconnected ecosystem of moving parts, personalities, and peculiarities.

Add into that three distinct meal periods, a whole service catering operation, and the full integration of a job training program—to say this was going to be complicated would be an understatement. And yet, it works. Most of the time.

We figured out efficient systems for delivering water to tables and storing silverware roll-ups and glasses. We perfected the rhythm of moving food and guests out to the patio, learning to walk and strut confidently. The next challenge was accommodating events and show nights. Located less than a mile away, The Bushnell Center for the Performing Arts hosted Broadway plays and large traveling shows. Firebox had been a primary dining spot before shows, and we were set to reclaim that status. Managing over 100 covers, cycling in and out with the expectation of four-star service within an hour, was daunting. Fortunately, my previous experience at a music venue allowed me to adapt proven systems to meet these demands efficiently.

And then the regular dinner crowd came in.

CHAPTER TWENTY FIVE

WIN, LOSE, WIN

People were excited, and I was thrilled to be back in Hartford. We were beginning to find our rhythm. The food was fresh, exciting, and innovative. Our cocktails were well-crafted, fun, and visually appealing. However, service was our greatest challenge. Despite being new, our staff sincerely cared for our guests, which resonated. They were fully committed to our program and mission, and this commitment helped compensate for some service shortcomings. But it was clear we needed improvement.

Additionally, the challenge of managing three meal services led to silos within the team. Exhausted from the energy-intensive opening, I struggled to effectively unite our team of over fifty members. While my managers and chefs were talented and passionate, their lack of experience showed. It didn't help that we had run through two executive chefs in a short time. Still, I couldn't use that as an excuse. I knew better and had managed better in the past, but fatigue was taking its toll this time.

So, where's the good news? The good news is that the foundation was strong. We had a solid base from which to build. But I knew we had to deliver. As a leader, I needed to be strong and level-headed, holding people accountable while showing compassion. Another good news was that I finally had a paid time off (PTO) job—something rare in our industry. Giving your life is almost expected, though no owner will ever say that. Being able to take some time to rejuvenate was precisely what I needed. Taking time off was a new and somewhat foreign concept, but I've realized its importance. I'm more effective and provide better leadership when I'm at my best—and I would say the same for my team. As we started implementing systems and training, some staff stayed on while others chose to leave, whether by their decision or ours. Through this process, we built our core team and became more cohesive.

What came next was quite a surprise. We had only been open a few months when the buzz about the Crazies awards began. Hosted by the Connecticut Restaurant Association, these awards are a big deal in the local scene. Rumors started circulating about us potentially being nominated for Best New Restaurant. This was astonishing, considering the competition involved hundreds of eligible restaurants across Connecticut, yet only five would make the ballot. We were incredibly new—were we even worthy? On one hand, yes, but deep down, I knew we weren't quite there yet. We might have seemed ready to the average guest, but I knew the truth. As thrilling as it would be to make the shortlist, I wasn't holding my breath.

The day the nominees were to be announced arrived shrouded in secrecy with no hints about who might be nominated. The announcements were to be streamed live on various social media platforms. Curiosity got the better of me, so I tuned in, thinking, "Well, you never know."

I was at my aunt and uncle's house for dinner, and my aunt was more thrilled about the potential nomination than I was. We ate, we toasted, and we watched. The nominees across all categories were impressive—renowned restaurants, chefs, and restaurateurs.

Then, it was time for our category: Best New Restaurants. They announced the first three nominees, and I began to resign myself to a "maybe next year" mindset, reminding myself that we would still be eligible. But then I heard it. "Fire by Forge." I was stunned. There we were, only six months into our journey, and we were nominated. I immediately started making calls and sending texts. My aunt was over the moon with excitement. I remembered the awards from six years prior when I had taken home the gold—one of the best nights of my life. Now, I had the chance to share this moment with my team. Perhaps this nomination was precisely what we needed to come together and feel like a family.

I was thrilled to share the news at the next pre-shift meeting: We were headed to the Crazies. Looking around at our large staff, I realized that aside from Ben and myself, no one had experienced the pomp and circumstance of such an honor. Many of our staff were from the city and had never left it. They had no idea what was in store. Ben had worked magic, persuading the board and several generous donors to provide a bus for our trip and secure four tables so the entire staff could partake in the festivities. An impressive 80% of our team committed to joining us for this prestigious industry event at the casino. It felt like our very own Oscar's night.

We all convened at the restaurant, awaiting the bus to transport us to the event. The excitement we'd built was palpable; everyone arrived dressed in their finest—suits, gowns, even tuxedos. For many, it was the first time they'd been the focus of such a celebration. Tonight, they would be. During cocktail hour, industry professionals from across the state mingled—vendors, restaurants, pastry chefs, bartenders, servers, and executive chefs, with thousands of our peers in attendance. Our restaurant alone brought a squad of 40, the excitement etched on their faces. The photo booth was constantly bustling with our team, perfectly capturing my envisioned unity.

As we sat at our assigned tables, the food and wine started to come out. We were treated to the hospitality that we dole out day in and day out. Angel, one of our former trainees, was now with the team. He was filming everything, walking around, and directing like he was making a feature film. At that moment, it hit me harder than ever. We are part of the process of changing lives. This was the win. At these tables was the victory.

The program started, and the awards were handed out. Many of the recipients were friends of mine, well-known industry figures, and up-and-comers—a fantastic lineup. However, as our category approached, I started to feel unexpectedly nervous. Although just being nominated felt like a stroke of luck, a part of me wondered if we might win. My competitive nature kicked in, heightening the tension. The announcement seemed to drag on forever. Finally, they announced the winner—it wasn't us, but a very deserving restaurant in the southern part of the state. I stood up quickly, clapping loudly. Looking back, I expected to see disappointment, but there they were—my team of 40, cheering enthusiastically along with me. They were fully present, thrilled to be part of the event and together as a team.

In the days that followed, the restaurant buzzed with stories and shared photos from the event. Our team had solidified and united by mission, profession, and a sense of duty. Angel and I exchanged a meaningful fist bump, acknowledging our collective journey. The starting point doesn't dictate where you end. We have a long way to go to our destination, but I feel confident that the bus we are on is going in the right direction.

EOD

END OF DAY

Credit: Lisa Nichols

I remember not long ago, a guest whom I met many years ago—seven restaurants back—came into my current spot. She began to share a story about her parents, who were regulars at a restaurant where I worked. I knew their preferences: what they ate, how they liked it, the timing, the jokes they enjoyed, and every other nuance that enhanced their dining experience.

After I opened the pizza bar, they followed my career and always visited my new spots. When the man sat down one evening, I realized I didn't have the cognac he always drank. He was particular about his cognac, never wavering. He didn't even want to hear the pitch.

I had a rum that I believed he would enjoy based on its aromas of orange peel, toffee, and licorice, and its refined, smooth taste. Needing to be creative, I brought it out, poured a little for him, his wife, and his daughter, and mentioned I just got it and was eager for their thoughts. He loved it, drank it all night, and it became his new regular choice, replacing the cognac. I opened a couple more restaurants after that, and the story slipped my mind until his daughter, visiting again after her father's passing, recounted how, on the day he passed, they all toasted with a bottle of that same rum, which he had purchased after that night at my bar. She told me how my hospitality would always be part of his story. That touched me deeply. We make an impact when we do it right. And I have a million more stories like this, as do all of us who are professionals. Never underestimate the effect we can have.

Writing this book has been a hell of a ride. I look back at all the lessons learned from the countless screw-ups, and it's comforting to know those blunders weren't in vain. Here I sit, with a decent paycheck, paid time off, health insurance, and get this—a daughter on the way. Somehow, I've been blessed with the knack to learn from my missteps, to forgive those who screwed me over, and to spot bullshit from a mile away. I'm quite a bit older now, a well-aged bottle of wine, finally ready to uncork. And I'm still learning every damn day.

Three decades deep, I'm still bussing tables, mixing drinks, chatting up guests, running food, scrubbing dishes, and coaching staff—sometimes all in one shift. It hasn't gotten old yet. That's the love affair I have with this business. I'm in a position not just to mentor trainees and staff but to be the best parent I could ever hope to be—something unfathomable if not for the restaurant business. I have so much love for this club.

This industry has evolved since I started at 17, especially post-COVID. The meritocracy is real. Hospitality is a genuine craft, an actual trade. I could have been a decent chef or a well-known bartender if I'd stuck with either. But life had other plans, making me the captain of this ship. It's not a glamorous gig, and often, you're doing the tough stuff without much reward—apart from the benefits, salary, and vacation time, which is pretty cool. But I'll never be just an office guy; the office is a coffin. Meetings? It's not where I shine. I thrive on the floor where I live—service to service. Each one is its episode, none to be taken for granted.

I can size up a guest before they even glance at the menu.

Step into any restaurant, and you can spot good or bad operators if you pay attention. You'll never catch on if we're hungover or having a crap day. The show goes on; the fourth wall stands firm. Walk into any bar I have ever run, and you would have never felt alone—unless you're a creep. Restaurants are like grocery store parking lots: they reveal people's true nature. Do you return your shopping cart? How do you treat the restaurant staff? Do you occupy multiple parking spaces? Do you falsely claim an allergy? These situations test your true character. This holds for restaurant staff as well. Do you ignore a dirty table because it's not in your section? Do you serve a dish with the burnt side down, hoping no one will notice? Under pressure, your true self emerges. Absolute professionals in our industry excel in these moments. Hospitality is another form of music.

A genuine professional embraces *omotenashi*, the cherished Japanese principle of hospitality that centers on warmly welcoming and caring for guests with genuine kindness and attentiveness. Commonly regarded as "wholehearted hospitality" or "selfless service," *omotenashi* is driven by three principles: meticulous attention to detail, anticipating the needs of others, and exceeding expectations to create a memorable experience. This is our ethos. While quick, transactional service might suffice for some, transcending to the level of *omotenashi* marks the beginning of a distinguished career where excellence is achieved and sustained.

I am not a celebrity chef. I am not a famous food writer. I am not a fancy mixologist. I am an old line cook who figured out how to have one foot in the spirit world and live in the world most people walk in. This field has breathed life into my experiences, offering adventure and enlightenment. It has equipped me with the tools to be the father my daughter deserves, the partner Sam needs, and the mentor I aspire to be for those who have washed up on the shores of our industry.

I have been sidelined by crushing depression, lost, and then found again. To rediscover myself, I had to return to my roots—to a time before the world had hardened me. Hospitality served as a lighthouse, guiding me back to safety. Now, much more a warrior, I have found peace. I have survived, so far. If I had to run it back, I would do it again. I have a shift tonight.

SIDE QUEST 1

ACROSS COUNTRY — 1994 - AGE 19

At 19, I didn't have much of a plan. Survival and taking each day as it came were my only strategies; I was good at executing them. AJ and I left Tampa intending to return in a few days. The plan was simple. Drive 876 miles to sell some cologne and perfume. AJ could visit her mom, and we can return. Easy peasy.

Upon reaching AJ's place, we headed straight to her VW Orange Bug. She revealed it was a 1975 model—ironically, the same year I was born. Proudly, she lifted the back to show the engine, pointing out a pencil, duct tape, and even a sock holding some hoses together. Being young and clueless about cars, I had no idea this vehicle was ill-prepared for the 3,000-mile journey ahead.

AJ also casually mentioned that she had swapped in a license plate from another registered orange VW Bug, assuring me that everything was set for our trip. I happily accepted this and didn't give it another thought.

We were off. I had brought my new Weezer cassette—*Blue Album*—and a Blues Traveler tape. It was a fun ride. We even sold a couple of bottles of eau de toilette allotted to us by the company to pay for a hotel room. She was good at her job, which explained why she was a boss at such a young age.

We made it to Louisville, and her mom, who managed a craft store, offered us some work to make a few extra bucks before returning. When our stint was up, I asked AJ, "Since we're up in Kentucky, how about we pop into Connecticut?" She agreed. Ironically, the trip from Tampa to Louisville was only four miles shorter than heading to Connecticut.

We hit Connecticut, and I caught up with all my friends and family, sharing tales of my latest escapades. No one was surprised by my return—I've always had a nomadic streak. They even bought a couple of bottles from us but didn't miss a chance to point out the folly of my involvement in what they deemed a crazy pyramid scheme. After a couple of days, I was restless again. Casually, I asked AJ if she wanted to go cross-country. I had family in Texas and California, and without hesitation, she agreed. Our preparation was minimal: just a few cases of imitation cologne and perfume.

My mother's neighbor at the time was a 60-year-old Jamaican truck driver, towering at 6'5" and weighing over 300 pounds. He was among the most remarkable and wisest men I'd ever met. AJ and I would often drop by to smoke a joint and chat. He didn't try to stop us when he learned of our plan to travel across the country. Instead, he offered advice that stuck with me: "If you own a map, you own the world." That was over 30 years ago. He handed us his road atlas of the U.S.—this was long before the days of GPS or MapQuest. Inspired, we painted our car like a couple of hippies and hit the road.

We had a good time, and the map proved invaluable. Although we were short on money, we managed to sell enough perfume to afford food and gas. However, we often had to sleep in the car. Being young, fear was a foreign concept, and the discomfort was far less than it would be now. Our journey took us through New York, Pennsylvania, Ohio, Indiana, Missouri, and Arkansas. Hot Springs was a standout—honestly, the only notable stop aside from the unique slice of Americana we experienced in each state. Life varied greatly from place to place, offering fantastic, albeit not thrilling, lessons. I'm sure we made a very similar impact.

Our luck selling our wares was mixed in these states, so we occasionally asked for spare change for gas outside fast food joints or gas stations. Being young and with AJ's charm, we managed well enough. For food, we targeted all-you-can-eat buffets and asked for leftovers before they were thrown out. Most staff were indifferent teenagers, so we usually succeeded. We did it on the down low to avoid making it a scene. Somehow, we were making it work.

We drove, stopped when we felt like it, followed the map to wherever we felt like going, and we just lived the way we felt day by day. We finally made it to Texas. My grandfather lived right outside Houston. It was also, ironically, my birthday. I thought he might be happy to see us. I got his address from calling my aunt collect. She did warn him of our arrival. We showed up and did not get a warm welcome. I remember him spending hundreds of dollars on lottery tickets and scratch-offs and asking us when we would leave. In hindsight, he probably was wondering what the plan was for these hippie kids not doing anything with their lives. He said happy birthday, handed me a 50-dollar bill, and sent us on our way. I was okay with the 50 dollars, and we took off.

On our journey through Texas, we made a detour to Waco. It had been just over a year since the infamous Waco siege, a tense standoff between U.S. federal and Texas state law enforcement and the Branch Davidians, a religious cult. Curiosity led us to the site of the former compound. We parked nearby and walked right up to what remained—fences around the perimeter could not keep out the eerie sense of history. The scene was surreal, just like the images broadcasted on TV: a bus and the rubble of buildings. An older woman approached us, mentioning she lived nearby. She warned that we were being watched and advised us to leave. Though she seemed a bit eccentric, at 19, I didn't fully grasp the significance of the site we were trespassing on.

We heeded her advice and left, but not before I impulsively took a door hinge from the ruins. Ironically, from that moment on, our journey began to take a turn for the worse.

As we neared the New Mexico border, visible in the distance, we were pulled over for the first time. I was a sight myself, with long hair and pot leaf tie-dyed T-shirt. At that moment, I was aware of a warrant for my arrest in Connecticut for failure to appear, a small amount of pot likely hidden somewhere in the back seat, and the realization that AJ's license was suspended—I didn't even have a license myself. Quickly, I swapped my shirt for a plain white tee I grabbed from the back seat.

The state troopers approached and requested the usual—license and registration. I admitted to not having a license or ID. They inquired about drugs; we denied having any. When they asked to search the car, our youthful naivety led us to consent. They rummaged through our belongings—cologne, perfume, random clothes—but found nothing incriminating. They then questioned our destination, and I told them we were headed to see my sister in Arizona. "You're five miles from the state border. Get in your car and make sure you leave Texas," one officer advised, hinting that our car would likely attract more attention.

Adding to our embarrassment, the car needed a push start. I pushed the car in front of the troopers until it coughed to life. Climbing in, AJ and I exchanged nervous smiles and sped off, relieved yet anxious about the rest of our journey. The only thing I can think now is they knew we would be someone else's problem.

We arrived in Carlsbad, New Mexico, and were greeted by picturesque southwestern rocky hills dotted with cacti. Out of nowhere, AJ suggested we stop for a climb. We pulled over at a makeshift roadside stop, and the road was elevated and surrounded by desert rocks and cacti. Ill-equipped for hiking, without proper clothing or shoes, and oblivious to the potential dangers of poisonous snakes, mountain lions, or scorpions, we began our ascent. Fortunately, our climb was safe and free from any things that may want to kill us. Reaching the summit, we paused to take in the expansive southwestern landscape bathed in the warm glow of the setting sun. It was perfect.

When we descended from our climb, I braced myself to push-start the car, but we faced uphill—a challenging setup. We needed to turn the car around, so AJ hopped into the driver's seat to steer while I pushed. The road was narrow, flanked only by a drop-off, making it difficult to maneuver. We couldn't turn sharply enough, and AJ leaped out to stop the car from going over the edge. Unfortunately, she couldn't stop it. The car tumbled down the five-foot embankment, and AJ vanished from sight. I heard a faint whimper and rushed to the edge.

There she was, lying amid cacti, with the car's front tire pinning her left leg. Without hesitating, I jumped down and tried to lift the car, managing to move it just an inch, but that only seemed to increase her pain. Realizing the quickest way to free her involved turning the wheel, I climbed into the driver's seat. This was going to hurt. The turn caused her to yelp in pain, but it worked—the tire rolled off her leg. Miraculously, aside from some scratches and a limp, she was okay.

Here came the rangers and with them, a flurry of questions. They checked if we were okay and if we needed an ambulance. AJ, tough as nails, declined, knowing we couldn't afford any delays. They scrutinized her more thoroughly since she was listed as the driver. Questions about the mismatched license plate and her suspended license followed. By the end of the ordeal, they laid out the consequences: our car would be towed and impounded. We'd need to sort out the legal details and settle fines to retrieve it.

For the moment, their solution was to drop us at the nearest rest stop as dusk settled in. This place was the epitome of sketchy—probably the most redneck rest stop I'd ever seen, even to this day. Groups loitered around pickup trucks, trailers dotted the area, and folks who looked rougher than us lounged around or camped in tents. There was a payphone there, so I called my aunt to let her know our whereabouts, half-joking that it might be the last time she'd hear from me. She was not amused. Understanding the gravity of the situation better than two teenagers could, she and my uncle quickly booked us a room at a budget hotel and urged us to find a ride there. We approached some less intimidating locals and, thankfully, hitched a ride. After over three weeks on the road, the promise of a real bed and a hot shower felt miraculous. At least, for that moment, it was.

AJ contacted some acquaintances who quickly doctored the necessary documents and faxed them to a nearby library. We picked them up and headed to the impound lot. The attendant there hadn't yet received the full rundown from the rangers, so he was somewhat unprepared for our story. We struck fast, glossing over the accident and explaining that the car had been impounded pending paperwork verification—which we conveniently had in hand. With the confidence of two kids who had neatly completed their school assignments, we convinced him. Selling was second nature to us after peddling knockoff cologne and perfume. He handed over the keys without a word. It was amazing.

I pushed the car to start it, and we took off, heaving a huge sigh of relief as we left the lot. "Let's call it quits while we're still ahead. Back to Connecticut?" I suggested. AJ agreed without hesitation. We plotted our route home, ready to close this wild chapter.

At this point, gas was getting harder to come by, as was food. It was not as fun as the first part of the trip. The speedometer was broken, and it made a loud rattling noise. The passenger window would not roll up all the way. The radio did not work. It was just time.

After a few eventful days, we reached Tennessee, just 850 miles, a standard number, from our destination. As we crossed a bridge in Knoxville, the car began to slow down unexpectedly and stopped—its engine was on fire. We barely managed to pull over before the vehicle was engulfed in flames, fueled by the bottles of cologne and perfume inside. Fire engines and police cars arrived quickly. Fortunately, their questions focused more on safety than probing our circumstances too profoundly.

The firefighters took us to the local police/fire station to plan our next steps. Inside, I noticed a perfectly drawn chalk art of a Confederate flag on a giant chalkboard—an unsettling welcome. We sat in a room where an officer, who was also watching a Tennessee vs. UConn women's basketball game—a significant rivalry—offered us the use of a phone. AJ called her mom in Kentucky, which is just a few hours away. Instead of taking a bus to Connecticut, her mom agreed to get us after talking to the officer.

During our wait, the officer engaged us in casual conversation, unaware of my Connecticut origins—a detail I was inclined to keep to myself given the setting but eventually came clean. He commented on the "good folk" around Knoxville and then veered into a disturbing commentary on local race relations. "Do you see the girls' holding hands with them up there?" he asked, implying a stark contrast with his perceived racial norms. His words left me uneasy; this wasn't just something I'd heard about—it was honest and correct before me.

The tension broke when AJ's mom arrived, coinciding with the officer's friend coming to watch a World War II documentary. It was our cue to leave. While I can't say everyone from that area is like the officer, encountering his stark views firsthand profoundly sucked.

Eventually, I returned to Connecticut the same way I left, by bus, and AJ came with me. It was nice, but once we were off the road, the allure of adventure faded, and the realities of everyday life set in. We eventually went our separate ways. To this day, I have no idea where she is, but I'll never forget our trip and how fortunate we were to make it there and back safely.

SIDE QUEST 2

ACROSS THE POND – 1996 - AGE 21

I was temporarily staying with Paul and his family as I figured out my next steps. He mentioned that a cousin in Ireland was getting married, and it was customary for a family member to attend. Paul was chosen and invited me to tag along since he planned to tour Ireland and the U.K. for several months afterward. Of course, I jumped at the chance. I hurried to get a passport and save as much money as possible in 30 days. The ticket and the expedited passport fee consumed nearly all the money I saved. Another friend was also joining us on this adventure. After buying a backpack and a few other essentials, I had just over $400 left. Everyone knew that wasn't nearly enough, but I wasn't concerned. I had a round-trip ticket, so I was confident I could get home and sort out everything else once I was there.

We took off from JFK and landed in Ireland, which was my first trip outside the U.S. Our flight touched down at Shannon Airport in the western part of the country, and we grabbed a taxi to Limerick. The city was exactly as I'd imagined from movies and fairy tales—pubs, ancient churches, and fields dotted with sheep. Everywhere was lush green. We spent our first night in a bed and breakfast, as the wedding was the next day, and we needed to spruce up. With my hair nearly down to my waist and a generally unkempt appearance, I was hardly in wedding form, but I was welcomed nonetheless.

The wedding was fantastic—or "great crack," as they say. Before the ceremony, the father gathered all his children for a toast. There was an older brother, three younger sisters aged between 19 and 25, and the youngest, a boy 14. Each was handed a glass of whiskey—the water in the glasses varied, with the youngest's glass mostly water and the oldest's neat whiskey. We toasted, and with that, the evening began.

There I was, having a blast, and suddenly, I woke up in a tent alongside my two friends. Stepping out to stretch, I noticed the roadside camped us with three other tents nearby. This was perfectly fine in Ireland. I greeted our neighbors; they chuckled and returned the greeting. Back in our tent, I mentioned the odd looks I'd received. My friends then informed me that in my drunken haze the night before, I had stumbled over to one of their tents, urinated next to it, and then collapsed like a sack of potatoes just a step away. Embarrassed, I apologized, and we quickly packed up to continue our journey.

Where to next? There was no concrete plan. Cork was our first target. We stuck out our thumbs and started hitchhiking, amazed that people picked us up! It quickly became apparent that locals were naturally curious and enjoyed the company. After a brief stop in Cork for food and drinks, we pressed on, aiming to reach Rosslare Harbor to catch a ferry to England. Surprisingly, we made it to the ferry in under three hours. Traveling across this country was vastly different from crossing back home.

We discussed our next move before heading to Amsterdam, and Stonehenge was our top choice. An Englishman seated next to us, who resembled an unshaven Mel Gibson, overheard our conversation and chimed in. "Stonehenge is rubbish," he said, "You'll have much more fun in town." He revealed that he was a contract diver for National Geographic, among other outlets, and lived in Hull, our next stop. "Stay at my place tonight," he offered, "and you can catch the ferry to Amsterdam from there." Why not, we thought.

That night, we were fantastic, just as the diver had promised. The following day, we awoke to find he had prepared butter and cheese sandwiches for us—a new but surprisingly tasty dish. He also advised us to tell people we were Canadian since Canadians seemed warmly received more than American tourists at the time. However, we didn't hide our origins; we weren't typical American tourists. We were adventurers.

We boarded the ferry and set off for Amsterdam. Upon arrival, we were instantly overwhelmed. Cannabis cafes were everywhere, and the city buzzed with people on bikes and boats. It seemed every bar paid homage to The Doors, and we were at a loss for where to begin. Our priority was finding accommodation, so we considered a hostel.

"Let's call timeout, go into a bar, smoke some weed, have a beer, and figure it out," one of us suggested. And that's precisely what we did. It was incredible. We chatted with a bartender who spoke English, and he tipped us off about a campground just a ten-minute walk from downtown. It was cheap, had showers, and all the signs in the city were in English, German, Dutch, and French.

On the way, we stopped at a bakery for a fresh loaf of bread and peanut butter, then hit a vending machine for some Grolsch beer—surprisingly available just like soda back home. Setting up our tent at the campground felt like joining an international village. We had neighbors from Scotland, England, Finland, and Germany—the Germans were into basketball, and the Scots enjoyed stirring up mischief.

After our Finnish neighbors mentioned a rave in town that evening, we decided to join them. Earlier in the day, we'd visited a magic mushroom shop where I bought a vial of yellow liquid. The clerk had assured me it would make me feel like I was flying, and that was all I needed to hear. As we headed out, I downed the vial.

"What does it feel like?" the Finnish kid walking with us asked.

"Like I'm flying," I replied, feeling a surge of energy from head to toe.

To this day, I still don't know what was in that vial.

The rave was held in an old factory, and each room had a different color and theme. I found myself in a room where the floor was made of rope. I lay down, mesmerized by the strobing lights on the ceiling, and to my surprise, one of the English girls from the campground walked in. Her scream of surprise echoed my excitement. She lay down next to me and asked how I was feeling. She was on something as well, as was everyone in the building. We spent hours there, and it was a fantastic night.

The next day, we decided to consume the mushrooms we'd bought, ignoring the clerk's advice to take only half. They were potent, and the trip was intense, heightened by the multilingual babble around us. When the Scots realized we were on our psychedelic journey, they joined in the fun, adding to the hilarity.

Eventually, we sobered up and explored the city further, visiting the Red-Light District, the Torture Museum, and more cannabis cafes. By the end of our stay, we knew it was time to leave, or we might never pull ourselves away.

We headed back to the U.K. After disembarking the ferry, we visited London, where Paul's cousin lived. We hitchhiked from the port, and my funds were nearly depleted. The others had brought three to four times as much money as I had. They toured the Tower of London, but I stayed outside, unable to justify spending my last bit of money on admission. Later, they grabbed some food at McDonald's. Starving, I reverted to my conman skills: I told the cashier they'd forgotten a burger and fries in my friend's order. Despite the manager's initial skepticism, my persistence (and volume) paid off—he handed over the food. It wasn't my proudest moment, but I was desperate. I even resorted to shoplifting eggrolls and other items from grocery stores. It was surprisingly easy, though I knew it wasn't a sustainable way to live.

As we sought directions to Paul's cousin's neighborhood at the bus station, a Somali woman overheard us discussing our slight confusion. After a brief chat, where we mentioned our plan to camp out, she advised against it in London and generously offered her backyard. Gratefully, we accepted her invitation and later met Paul's cousin and her English husband at a local pub. The conversation turned tense when Oliver Cromwell appeared—Paul labeled him a murderer, while the cousin's husband hailed him as a hero. The bar fell silent, and suddenly, everyone had an opinion. It was an unexpectedly intense night that gave me a glimpse into regional tensions reminiscent of those back home, except with a 1000-year difference.

That night, we returned to the Somalian Samaritan's house and set up our tent in her backyard. The following day, she offered for us to come up and eat breakfast with her family. They had made beans and bread. It was the most generous thing I can remember from our trip. It was a wonderful experience and conversation.

We were now off to visit the girl from South Carolina in Cambridge.

We hitched several rides and finally arrived in Cambridge. Our new friend managed to sneak us into her dorm room, which was cramped for four people but still better than a tent. Lacking a sleeping bag, I was grateful for the indoors despite only having a thin blanket I'd swiped from a ferry, which barely covered me.

In the dorm, we met our neighbors, three Italians, and spent an evening enjoying homemade meals and pints together. Paul and Carolina quickly hit it off, and soon, Paul would shed his virgin status, proving the bird's droppings on our departure indeed were a stroke of good luck.

After settling in for a week, I decided to look for work. Eventually, I spoke with a chef who needed a dishwasher and prep cook. I assured him I could handle both roles and lived just down the street. His main concern was my lack of a work visa, but I promised him it was being sorted and suggested he pay me in cash.

I started working that weekend. Beyond washing dishes, I learned to make leek soup and Yorkshire pudding, crafted lamb burgers, and explored other new cuisines. It was a fantastic experience, capped off by having pints with the staff after shifts. By the second weekend, having just received my pay, I was about to have the room to myself. My friends had left for the Phoenix Festival in Stratford-upon-Avon, a four-day event established in 1993 by John Vincent Power of the Mean Fiddler Music Group as an alternative to the traditional Glastonbury and Reading festivals.

When I returned to the dorm, the door was locked. Lacking a key and not officially supposed to be there, I couldn't just ask the superintendent to let me in. Stranded with my friends off at a festival for the next few days, I felt utterly alone. What was I supposed to do now? I knew no one, my belongings were locked inside the room, and camping wasn't an option.

With only a few dollars to my name, I thought, "What the hell," and decided to find out where the festival was held, hitchhike there, and sneak in to find my friends. Simple, right? Except it was over 100 miles away in a foreign country. MapQuest didn't exist, nor did I have a cell phone, and thousands of people were in attendance. On a whim, I was about to embark on an epic journey.

I stopped by a local liquor store, bought a pint, and asked for a piece of cardboard and a marker. After scrawling "Stratford-upon-Avon" on the cardboard, I headed to the nearest highway on-ramp.

I was picked up and soon on my way. My journey to Stratford-upon-Avon, the medieval market town and the birthplace of William Shakespeare, was marked by a series of wild rides: a maniac from the French Foreign Legion, a cyclist from the Tour de France, and about three others before I reached the outskirts of town.

Stratford-upon-Avon, nestled in England's West Midlands, is renowned as the 16th-century birthplace of possibly the most famous writer in the English language. Shakespeare's legacy includes timeless sonnets and plays like *Romeo and Juliet* and *Hamlet*. The Royal Shakespeare Company celebrates his work, performing regularly at the Royal Shakespeare Theatre and the adjacent Swan Theatre along the River Avon.

When I reached the outskirts, the road was isolated, flanked by sheep fields without street lights or houses. As dusk turned to darkness, I was ready to bed in a field when a car passed and stopped ahead of me. The driver reversed, rolled down the window, and asked where I was headed. "I'm trying to get to the Phoenix Festival," I told him. "Hop in," he replied, his kindness apparent as I climbed into the back seat next to a baby in a car seat while his wife sat up front.

"My brother is an EMT at the festival," he explained as we drove towards the bustling site filled with cars, police, and festival-goers. I confessed I didn't have a ticket and needed to sneak in. Pulling over a mile from the entrance, he offered to help. We said goodbye to his wife and child, then dashed through the fields under moonlight, leaping over streams and navigating fences until we reached the back of the festival site.

The makeshift fence, set on a stone base, was easy to lift. He hoisted it just enough for me to roll underneath. I shook his hand in gratitude, thanked him for his incredible help, and never saw him again.

I thought I was in, until I realized I was just in the parking lot. At least I was closer to the action. A wild group of rowdy young Englishmen called me over as I walked further. They were planning to sneak in and invited me to join. "Follow us, Captain America, we have a plan," they joked, hearing my accent.

We approached the ticket entrance, where they bluffed to security, claiming they were the IT team hired for a job. After we were ushered past the checkpoint, the guards asked for credentials. The group entered a booth but soon came back out. "Sorry, we don't have you on our list," the guards said. As the group leader started to argue, I noticed a bunch of kids preparing to sprint toward the fence. Suddenly, over a dozen people were climbing it. The wall gave way, and I seized the moment to dash.

About half a mile behind the main stage, I ran for my life. As I ran, Neil Young played "Keep On Rocking in the Free World," probably 1000 feet before me. Fireworks were going off, and I was dodging security flashlights and hearing dogs bark. Some of my fellow escapees paused, but I kept going, diving down a hill to avoid the lights. Regaining my footing, I ran along the fence until I spotted a small hole and quickly squeezed through it.

On the other side, I found a group of long-haired youths passing around a joint. I quietly joined their circle, blending in just as security swept through. They didn't give me a second glance, likely missing a clear view of me during my sprint. Once again, I thought, "Now, I'm really in."

I wandered around, noting vendors, thousands of people, and countless tents. When I asked where the show was, I learned it was beyond another checkpoint; I had only reached the campground, not the actual concert grounds. It was getting late, so I decided to secure a sleeping spot and attempt to enter the concert area in the morning. Spotting a couple of kids by a fire, I asked if I could join them. I still had the pint I bought earlier and figured it was the perfect time to open it. After sharing drinks and stories with them around the fire, I drifted off to sleep.

Waking up to the warm sun was glorious. However, the reality quickly set in: I was over 100 miles away from anything familiar, and my friends were somewhere beyond the next fence among thousands of festival-goers. What was my next move? With only 10 pounds in my pocket and growing hunger, I debated whether to spend my last money on food or beer. As I wandered, deep in thought, a familiar voice suddenly called out, "JUSTIN?! What the hell are you doing here?" It was my friends. I couldn't believe it—I had found them, or they had seen me. Laughing, I shared my tale. They had tickets for the concert. "You need them to get in," they said. "I'll meet you inside somehow," I replied, determined.

I met three guys scalping tickets priced precisely at the 10 pounds in my pocket. I bought one and tried to enter the concert, but the ticket was fake. Spotting the guys attempting to hustle another group, I confronted them. As one began to circle behind me, I raised my voice to draw attention. Reluctant to attract a crowd, they quietly refunded my money and urged me to leave.

Afterward, I struck up a conversation with a friendly Belgian security guard. She was charming, and I casually inquired about the best way to sneak into the concert. As we talked, she mentioned that volunteers could work and attend the event. Excited, I followed her directions and filled out the paperwork, but I hit a snag when I asked for my passport, which was back in the dorm room in Cambridge. All I had were my clothes and 10 pounds.

Returning to the guard, I played with her new plan. "Did your wristband get stolen?" she asked. Playing my part, I exclaimed, "Yes! Someone just ripped it off and ran!" We exchanged knowing smiles. She radioed for backup, and another guard joined us, being informed that he'd seen the thief. This guard escorted me to the checkpoint, briefed the staff, and I was quickly equipped with a new wristband and ushered through the gates.

Finally, inside, for real, I reunited with my friends. We enjoyed performances by Prodigy, Bjork, Cypress Hill, and many others. It was an unforgettable experience.

Paul and Carolina had train tickets, but I didn't, so my friend, wanting an adventure of his own, decided to join me on the hitchhiking journey home. Amidst the hundreds of cars and the sea of people, we quickly caught a ride to the town center. Our benefactors were a dentist driving the car and a hippie girl in the passenger seat. Unfortunately, the car broke down shortly after, forcing us to pull over on a hot roadside.

The girl explained that she had just met the dentist and was hitching a ride. We had chatted in the car, and I was careful not to be too flirtatious, unsure of her relationship with the driver. Eventually, she suggested we walk down to a nearby horse barn to find some water. Leaving my friend with the dentist, we walked down to the barn. There, we found a hose and started drinking. The mood lightened when she playfully sprayed water on both of us. We talked a bit more and then walked back to the car. It was only much later that I realized she had been interested in me, and the walk had been her way of making our interaction more playful. Being young and shy, I hadn't picked up on her cues.

We eventually found alternative rides and returned to Cambridge, where we stayed a couple more days before setting off to explore Scotland.

Scotland was breathtakingly beautiful; the people were wild and fun, and the food was delightful—full of good beer and great whisky. We were heading to see a friend in Carlisle, a town on the Scotland-England border. We had met her in the States, and she'd offered us a place to stay if we were ever in the area. By the time we arrived, it was too late to drop in. In those days, we decided to wait out the night without everyone having a cell phone. We wandered through the quiet town looking for a public space to pitch our tent, and there it was—Carlisle Castle.

Carlisle Castle is a medieval stone keep fortress near Hadrian's Wall's ruins. Initially built during the reign of William II in 1092 and later rebuilt in stone under Henry I in 1122, the castle is over 930 years old and has witnessed numerous pivotal events in British history. It played a significant role in the Wars of Scottish Independence and was the last English fortress to undergo a siege during the Jacobite Rising of 1745–46. The castle had been listed as a Scheduled Ancient Monument just six days before our arrival.

Camping outside the castle, we felt a connection to all those who had laid siege to the fortification nearly a thousand years earlier. It was a surreal and memorable experience.

We made it to the home of our English friend, Casey, who lived with her dad. They graciously welcomed us. After drinking more tea than I had ever consumed, Casey took us around town, proudly showing us off to her friends as if we were new puppies. That night, we all went out to the local club, a popular hangout for young people from the border towns of England and Scotland. It was the primary source of entertainment in the area.

The night was enjoyable until Casey and some friends suggested we leave before the club closed. While half the room was thrilled to learn about the visiting American boys, the other half was not as welcoming. There was talk of potential fights at closing time, so we left early with our group. Suddenly, one of the girls from the club grabbed my arm and pulled me into her taxi— I was kidnapped. Thankfully, it was someone I had been chatting with.

The taxi took us to her house. It was 2 a.m., and I thought we'd sneak in quietly, but instead, she dragged me into the backyard and her shed. "My dad will kill you if he finds out you're here, so we need to be quiet," she whispered. I woke up with my head resting on a lawn mower and managed to sneak out early enough to catch a taxi back to Casey's. All three of us had similar adventurous tales from after the club. No wonder half the guys in town didn't want us there.

The next day, Casey's dad took us all to Hadrian's Wall. This former defensive fortification of the Roman province of Britannia, begun in A.D. 122 during the reign of Emperor Hadrian, runs from Wallsend on the River Tyne in the east to Bowness-on-Solway in the west. As a history buff, visiting the wall, a massive stone barrier with large ditches on either side that spanned the island's width, was an incredible experience.

As our time abroad drew to a close, we said our goodbyes and hitchhiked to the ferry back to Ireland, arriving in Dublin. The city was vibrant, and we explored a few pubs before quickly realizing that camping in the city wouldn't be as feasible as in smaller towns. A helpful bartender suggested we take the train to the outskirts, where it would be easier to find a camping spot. Heeding his advice, we boarded the train that night and disembarked at the last stop. It was pitch dark.

We began exploring and soon found ourselves walking through trees lining the road, which opened up to a glorious field. The soft grass overlooking the water, with a castle shimmering under the moonlight, seemed too good to be true. A solitary tree was in the middle of this picturesque landscape, where we set up our tent. It was a perfect night's sleep on the comfy grass.

The following day, as I stretched outside the tent, the daylight revealed our proper location: we weren't in any random field but on a meticulously groomed golf course. I spotted three older gentlemen in golf attire approaching; we were right in the middle of their game. Quickly waking my friends, we packed up as fast as possible and headed back to the city. Despite the mix-up, camping on that golf course was perfect.

While in the city, reflecting on our trip over a pint as we awaited our flight home, I suddenly realized, "OH SHIT! My passport must have fallen out in that girl's shed in Carlisle." If it were today, I could text her to send it to me. But it was 1996. I didn't have her last name, address, or phone number. After a brief moment of panic, I headed to the embassy. Remarkably, I was seen relatively quickly. I told them my story, and they laughed, offering to issue a temporary passport for $100. As broke as I was, but they agreed I could pay later, to which I consented.

That night, we boarded our plane home. I looked and felt like a homeless person after living rough for the last two months. Yet, by another stroke of luck, a flight attendant passed me a note: one of her colleagues thought I was cute and offered to buy us a round. I said I also found her attractive and would love a drink. We drank for free for the entire flight home, and I even got her phone number. She lived in Chicago. However, I decided to hold off on any further adventures for a while.

SIDE QUEST 3

BUSKING THE SYSTEM — 2011 - AGE 31

My friend Nick and I were venturing into video production. Armed with editing equipment, a brand-new Panasonic digital camera, and many ideas, we were scraping by with local commercials and small video shoots. These gigs paid the bills, but I was itching to scratch a creative itch. While living in NYC, I was captivated by the subway musicians' exceptional talent. Some, I discovered, earned a substantial income. Driven by curiosity, I figured this was the perfect subject for a documentary. Alongside Nick and a well-read friend from my restaurant job who was eager to jump in on the writing, we embarked on creating *Busking the System.*

The documentary aimed to delve into the diverse lives of several subway musicians in the city. We followed three green musicians tracking their attempts to carve out careers in the challenging environment of the New York subway. Will they find success or fade into obscurity? The film also features a musician who has already made a name for himself in the subway scene and contrasts his story with the grittier reality of a man who performs solely to survive. From uplifting idealism to the harsh truths of the underground, *Busking the System* shines a light on the lives behind the music echoing through the subway tunnels.

We began by searching for three distinct musicians. After placing an ad on Craigslist and reviewing video submissions, we discovered Nate, a dynamic rock band leader from Cleveland. Then there was Matt, a seasoned blues guitarist in his thirties from Seattle, and Phillip, a driven musician in his late twenties from Kansas City. Each brought a unique style, personality, and ambition.

Our young camera operator, Jackson, was tasked with covering Matt. We sent him to Seattle to cover his travel expenses, including a plane ticket, food, and accommodations. His assignment also included a lengthy bus journey with Matt to NYC—a challenging assignment reflecting his junior status on our team.

Meanwhile, we enlisted Randy, a friend who had previously collaborated with us, to follow Nate in Cleveland. I headed to Kansas City to meet Phillip.

Equipped with our gear, we embarked on a week-long journey across different states.

My first impression of Missouri was of vast, empty fields dotted with hay rolls and surrounded by highways and strip malls featuring fast-casual dining. Upon meeting Phillip, the ambiance became more welcoming. The neighborhoods were meticulously planned, resembling crop circles in their perfect cul-de-sac arrangements—a stark contrast to the haphazard streets of the Northeast. I soon found out Missouri was pretty fucking cool.

At the time, Phillip had just started courting a girl, which added a charming dimension to his story. I wasn't sure how the other musicians were faring, but I was becoming quite familiar with Phillip. He was not only a nice guy but also a gifted musician. I recorded several of his shows, captivated by his solo performances that pulsed with groove and emotion. Despite his peaceful demeanor, a stark contrast to the bustling energy of NYC, I often wondered how long he could sustain performing in the subway stations.

We said our goodbyes and hopped on a bus to NYC, embarking on a journey that would take a few days. I hadn't done this since I was 19. The bus ride was taxing, and the bus stations were even worse—I had gone soft. By chance, during a layover in Scranton, Pennsylvania, I spotted Jackson. "Holy shit! What a coincidence," I exclaimed. Matt was with him but asleep. "Are you guys on our bus into NYC?" I asked. They weren't, which was a relief since I didn't want the two musicians to meet yet. It was good to catch up with Jackson, though he confessed he wasn't thrilled with his assignment. I couldn't contain a big laugh. "Why?" I asked. "This guy complains non-stop," he answered. "It's miserable. Being trapped on a bus with him is awful." "Almost done, my friend," I reassured him. We then boarded our separate buses and continued our journeys.

When we arrived in NYC, Phillip had arranged a temporary place to stay with someone his sister knew in Washington Heights, a long trek from Penn Station. He looked like a deer in headlights the whole time. We took the subway up to his temporary home, and I promised to return the next day to help him try busking, perhaps in a park. Afterward, I checked into my hotel room in Manhattan and met up with Jackson and Randy, who were staying in the same hotel. I realized then how soft I'd become; I loved the comfort of my bed and shower.

Randy updated me about Nate, who is brimming with energy and charisma and is highly eager to perform. We already knew about Matt—tough exterior but a constant complainer. Then there was Phillip, a somewhat naive singer-songwriter, timid about playing on the streets and harboring a romantic notion of how things should be.

As we set out, the musicians hit the streets to earn money through their performances. At the end of each day, we would gather to share stories. Phillip managed to make $5, Nate earned $20 and even got some phone numbers, while Matt just complained.

After a week, we began connecting with seasoned musicians and conducted several interviews. One memorable encounter was with Theo. I was drawn to his music and waited eagerly to hear his story after his performance. Originally from Austria, Theo had become a staple in the NYC subway scene, constantly playing and now fully integrated. He knew everyone, understood the unwritten rules, and spoke the language fluently, making him the perfect guide for our underground adventure.

One day, Jackson called me in a panic. "I can't find Matt," he said. "What do you mean you can't find him?" I asked. Jackson explained that Matt was supposed to meet him at 11, but hadn't shown up. When he checked Matt's place, he was told Matt had left—destination unknown. They didn't know where he went, and he wasn't answering his phone either. "Oh shit, did Matt get killed?" I wondered. This could turn into a very different kind of documentary. "Okay, let's just stay calm," I planned. "We'll hope he just jumped ship and follow up with his family in a day or so to see if they've heard anything."

As our research for the movie progressed, we learned about Larry Wright, a prominent New York City street performer born around 1975. Renowned for pioneering using five-gallon plastic buckets as drums, Wright innovatively lifts the bucket with his foot to alter sound patterns. His unique talent has led to appearances in commercials, Mariah Carey's "Someday" music video, the Broadway show *Bring in 'da Noise, Bring in 'da Funk*, and films like *Green Card*.

Wright's contributions to music include performing on the album *Ritual Beating System* by Bahia Black, produced in 2016 by Bill Laswell. The album consists of "Uma Viagen Del Baldes de Larry Wright" ("A Journey of Larry Wright's Buckets"), a track he co-wrote with Carlinhos Brown. Furthermore, his life and early years are depicted in an independent film focusing on his time as a high school student. Larry has been playing music since he was five years old.

"How do we find this guy? He has no website, social media, or agent; he's like a ghost." Discussing him with Theo made Larry seem even more like a character from a fairytale. "Oh, you won't find Larry unless he wants you to find him," Theo said, "but I can help you track him. You won't want to approach him alone." Though Theo tended to exaggerate, he was often accurate, which piqued my curiosity. I was all in—let's find Larry Wright.

I dedicated the day to exploring with Theo in search of Larry. We traversed the blue, red, and green subway lines. As we navigated the underground, Theo suddenly stopped and bent down to pick up paint chips. "He was here not long ago," he remarked, like a hunter inspecting signs of a bobcat. Despite our efforts and tips to try this station or that one, we had no luck finding him all day.

One day, while randomly following Phillip on his venture to play in the subways, I heard the faint banging of drums a few platforms away. I hurried toward the sound, Phillip in tow. As we descended the last set of stairs, the music grew louder, and to my delight, there was Larry Wright, jamming with a woman who I later learned was his wife. I waited until they finished their set, then tossed $20 into his box. I quickly introduced myself, aware that he had probably heard every pitch imaginable. I offered to pay for his time and handed him my number to arrange an interview and record his performance, trying not to pressure him too much. I left feeling exhilarated—Larry was honest, and he was incredible.

A few days later, Larry called. I eventually met him, his wife, and even their kids, who danced as they played buckets. It was like discovering an inner-city Von Trapp family.

That encounter was the pinnacle of my film. I wrapped up the movie a few weeks later. Of the original three, only Nate remained in NYC. We eventually learned that Matt had slipped away in the night, and Phillip had given up after a few weeks. Throughout the project, we met numerous talented musicians like the Saw Lady, who played, you guessed it, a saw; Shaker legs, a drummer who once opened for Guns N' Roses; and Billy Rogan, an incredible guitarist from Pennsylvania. The stories were fantastic, and I learned so much.

The documentary was completed and turned out great—or so I thought. We managed to get it into a few film festivals and screened it at art houses across the country. It was thrilling to travel with the movie and share the stories of these buskers on the big screen.

The royalties were negligible despite partnering with agents who placed the movie on several digital platforms. Although we recouped some of our investment, the project was primarily a financial loss, especially after accounting for all the travel and marketing expenses. Nonetheless, I was determined to use this experience as a springboard for my next project, titled *The Dark Side of the Stage*, which would explore the lives of comedians, echoing the adage of the "tears of a clown."

We interviewed Doug Stanhope, whom I opened up for at Foxwoods Casino, Artie Lange, Nick DiPaolo, and many other notable comedians. To truly grasp the concept, I even tried my hand at stand-up comedy. Bombing was an excruciatingly lonely feeling of failure, whereas killing on stage provided a tremendous high. We gathered many great hours of content, but life intervened unexpectedly, and I could not bring this project to fruition. Thus, my movie career ended, but my hospitality career was beginning. I made some noise, appeared on the big screen, took the stage, and even got my name on IMDb. The itch was scratched, and the lessons were learned. Now, it's time to focus on how I can be of service.

DRINK RECIPES

I. BESO ROJA

Credits: Leungevity Photography

SANGRIA FOAM MARGARITA

- 1.75 oz Tres Agaves Blanco Tequila
- 1 oz Lime juice
- .75 oz Triple Sec
- .25 oz Agave nectar

1. Shake with Ice
2. Hawthorne strain over ice
3. Add orange garnish

*RECIPE FOR SANGRIA FOAM

- 3 Egg Whites
- 2 oz Lemon
- 5 oz Joel Gott Cab
- 2 oz OJ
- 2 oz Triple sec

1. Combine ingredients into a whip cream cannister

2. FILTHY RICH

Credits: Leungevity Photography

- 2oz Hanson Habanero Vodka
- .25 oz Trinchieri Vermouth Dry

1. Stir over ice for 30-45 seconds until cold
2. Pour over cold martini glass
3. Add Srichacha Blue cheese bacon stuffed Olives

*BLACK GARLIC OLIVE OIL

- 1 black garlic clove chopped
- ¼ cup extra virgin olive oil

1. Shake and let rest for 1 day

*BLUE CHEESE BACON STUFFED OLIVES

1. Combine Blue Cheese, bacon, Sriracha in a blender or Robot Coupe to taste
2. Stuff into Pitted Spanish Queen Olives

3. **KISS FROM A ROSE** (Award Winning Cocktail from Chapter Thirteen)

Credits: Leungevity Photography

- 1.25 oz Highclere Castle Gin
- 1 oz Wild Moon Rose Liquor
- 1 oz Fresh Squeezed Grapefruit
- .75 oz Fresh Lemon Juice
- 4 dashes of fee foam

1. Shake and fine strain into a cold martini glass or coupe
2. Shake Rose Petal Powder over drink

4. OMOTENASHITNI

Credits: Leungevity Photography

- 1.75 oz Hanson Mandarin Vodka
- .75 oz Asian Pear Sake
- .25 oz Fruitful Triple sec
- .25 oz Lime Juice
- Splash Cranberry Juice
- dash Fernet Branca

1. Combine, shake and fine strain into cold martini glass
2. Garnish with a lime wheel

5. NIGHTRIDER

Credit: Lisa Nichols

- 1.5 oz Up n' Down Rock and Bourbon
- Fresh Shot of Espresso
- 0.50 oz Coffee Liqueur
- 0.25 oz Sweetened Liqueur (ex. Tuaca)
- Or simple syrup

1. Add Lemon Twist to Shaker
2. Shake Vigorously and fine strain into cold glass
3. Garnish Options: Espresso Beans, Lemon Twist, Chocolate Shavings, etc.

Our most popular UND cocktail, besides the Old Fashioned!

6. THE SECRETARIAT

Credit: Winter Caplanson

- Spank or muddle Mint
- 1.5 oz Up n' Down Rock and Bourbon
- 0.5 oz Lemon Juice

1. Shake
2. Pour Over Ice
3. Top w/ Ginger Ale
4. Garnish: Mint or Lemon

Refreshing + Delicious!

7. YUZU COWBOY

- 1 ½ oz Mezcal
- 1 oz Fruitful Yuzu Liqueur
- ¾ oz Agave Nectar
- ¾ oz Lime Juice
- ¾ oz Orange Juice

1. Add all ingredients into mixing tin and shake heartily
2. Double strain using the hawthorn and fine mesh strainers into double rocks glass
3. Garnish with dehydrated lime wheel and candied ginger

8. (CCCC) CALIFORNIA COAST CUCUMBER CRUSHER

- 2 oz Hanson Cucumber Vodka
- 1oz Lemonade
- .5 Lime Juice

1. Combine and shake
2. Strain over ice
3. Top with 2oz Avissi Prosecco
4. Garnish with a slice of cucumber

9. LOUISVILLE SOUR

Credits: Lisa Nichols

- 1.75 Up n' Down rock and bourbon
- 1 oz lemon juice
- .75 Fruitful watermelon Liqueur
- .25 or a dash of oj
- 5 dashes of fee foam

1. Dry shake wet shake
2. Fine strain into a cold martini glass
3. Angostura drops